To
Cindy
Gutierrez
from

Maranatha
Sandra Ramirez

7-18-21

PARABLES
and
PONDERINGS

SANDRA SHUMATE RAMIREZ

WESTBOW
PRESS®
A DIVISION OF THOMAS NELSON
& ZONDERVAN

Scripture taken from the New King James Version. Copyright © 1979, 1980, 1982 by Thomas Nelson, Inc. Used by permission. All rights reserved.

Scripture taken from the King James Version of the Bible.

Scripture taken from the Holy Bible, NEW INTERNATIONAL VERSION®. Copyright © 1973, 1978, 1984 by Biblica, Inc. All rights reserved worldwide. Used by permission. NEW INTERNATIONAL VERSION® and NIV® are registered trademarks of Biblica, Inc. Use of either trademark for the offering of goods or services requires the prior written consent of Biblica US, Inc.

Scripture quotations taken from the Holy Bible, New Living Translation, Copyright © 1996, 2004. Used by permission of Tyndale House Publishers, Inc., Wheaton, Illinois 60189. All rights reserved.

WestBow Press books may be ordered through booksellers or by contacting:

WestBow Press
A Division of Thomas Nelson & Zondervan
1663 Liberty Drive
Bloomington, IN 47403
www.westbowpress.com
1 (866) 928-1240

Because of the dynamic nature of the Internet, any web addresses or links contained in this book may have changed since publication and may no longer be valid. The views expressed in this work are solely those of the author and do not necessarily reflect the views of the publisher, and the publisher hereby disclaims any responsibility for them.

Any people depicted in stock imagery provided by Thinkstock are models, and such images are being used for illustrative purposes only.
Certain stock imagery © Thinkstock.

ISBN: 978-1-5127-0856-1 (sc)
ISBN: 978-1-5127-0857-8 (hc)
ISBN: 978-1-5127-0855-4 (e)

Library of Congress Control Number: 2015913175

Print information available on the last page.

WestBow Press rev. date: 9/30/2015

Contents

PONDERINGS

Introduction

Testimony of a Child

These writings show how death affected me and God's way of using even death to draw people to Him. There were people who welcomed me into their lives and hearts during my time of need. This is the beginning of my salvation story. I did not give a public testimony until my baby was eighteen years old. I did not want my children to know all I went through as a child until they were old enough to sustain the truth. Even now, there are private things I must keep because telling them would only hurt people. I have purposefully written as I remembered the events. I was a child, so the words are the words of a child. Please have patience with the childlike writing.

Once upon a time there was a little girl named Sandy. She had a pretty good childhood, a mom and dad who loved her, an older sister, and a younger sister. Her life went along uneventfully until she reached the age of eight. At age eight, her daddy died very unexpectedly.

Sandy didn't quite know how to take this. It was the first time in her life she had experienced the death of anyone. Her daddy just looked like he was sleeping, and if she looked really hard, she thought she could see him breathing.

She reached up and touched him. He didn't feel right. He was cold, and when she touched his chest on the place where she used to lay her head, she felt a hard, cold something that was very scary. She ran away to the other room and didn't touch him again. To this day, the stifling aroma of fresh carnations brings all those vivid memories back as if she were eight years old again.

She found out that when she went home, it didn't feel like home anymore. There was no routine. Dinners were not the same. There was no discipline, and as much as she thought it would be fun not to have discipline, she really missed it. She asked in her heart, *Daddy, Daddy, why did you leave me?*

Her mommy was not her mommy anymore. She forgot who she was and became a little girl in her mind. She hurt Sandy in ways that were not too understandable to an eight-year-old. Daddy used to keep Mommy in line and help her to cope with a life that was too much for Mommy. Her mommy never did quite grow up after that. Sandy asked again in her heart, *Daddy, Daddy, why did you leave me?*

At age eleven, Sandy was taken away from her home because of the lack of care and the abuse authorities found in that home. The authorities put Sandy and her older sister in jail! Sandy didn't know what she had done to be placed in jail. They locked the big steel doors and would not return, no matter how hard she cried or how loud she hollered for the policeman to return. Sandy asked in her heart, *Daddy, Daddy, why did you leave me?*

The policeman eventually returned and opened the cell door. The authorities had found a receiving home that would accept abused, neglected, and homeless little children. They drove Sandy and her sister there in a police car and dropped them off late at night. They gave no explanations and no apologies. Sandy's heart cried out in anger, *Daddy, Daddy, why did you leave me?*

There was a big, black housemama who took care of the receiving home. She got Sandy and her sister hot food, a bath, clean clothes, and their very own bed. She smelled like baby powder and was as gentle as a breeze. She was something called a Christian. Sandy was immediately drawn to her with her whole heart, but as a child, she did not understand why.

A week later, when Sandy returned from a field trip with the home's personnel and the other children, she noticed the big plate-glass window in the front of the receiving home had been broken. Sandy's heart sank. Violence, pain, and destruction were Mom's ways of coping with life. She knew her mom had been there and was going to take them away from this place she loved. A mixture of guilt for not wanting to go and fear at being taken home flooded Sandy's heart.

What Sandy didn't know was that the authorities had found her baby sister in an abandoned car and had brought her to the home. Sandy's mom found out where they were and had indeed come to get her three daughters. In her childlike way, Mommy loved her three daughters fiercely.

The authorities would not let them go. They took Sandy's mom to a state institution where she would get the medical help she needed to cope with the loss of her husband. The responsibility of three little girls just proved to be more than a twenty-nine-year-old childlike woman could cope with.

There was an incident once when Sandy heard a loud crash and the sound of breaking glass. Before she remembered where she was, she jumped out of bed, thinking that Mom had gotten angry for some reason. Sandy was going to get the baby out of harm's way. As she ran toward the sound, she realized she was in the receiving home and not at home. The fear went away, but curiosity got the best of her. She walked toward the noise.

What a sight! There stood that big, black housemama with her hands on her hips, looking at a huge tree branch that had crashed through the skylight of the receiving home. Glass was all around, and the rain was pouring in. She heard Sandy walk in, turned around, and looked her square in the eye. "Girl, what's you doin' outta bed? Go on, go on and get yosef back in that bed. Yo housemama done got evr thin' unner control. Ain't no chile needs to be worrin' about no grown people thin'! Go on, go on now. Shoo."

A feeling came over Sandy that she was not able to explain until she was much older. Such a peace and comfort that her housemama did indeed have everything under control. Nothing had been under control in Sandy's life for years. She didn't realize it then, but she had a role model. Someone she would want someday to be just like. Her housemama appeared strong, confident, under control, and encouraging. She seemed to have a strength that was greater than any problem and a love that included each and every young girl put in her care.

Sandy's relatives decided it would be best if the three little girls were placed with family members. Sandy went to live with an uncle, who was a preacher, in the state of West Virginia. She was very, very, happy there. It was quiet and peaceful. There was food all the time. She didn't have to cook, clothes she didn't have to wash and iron, and a clean bed to sleep in. There was no physical pain and no emotional abuse. Best of all, she got to be a kid again.

A few days before Palm Sunday in 1957, her uncle—or as Sandy called him, the Preacher—was studying to give his Easter message and called Sandy into the living room. "Sandy, listen to this: '*Eloi, Eloi, lama sabachthani.*' Do you know what that means?" Sandy shook her head. They were words in a language she had never heard before.

Her uncle said "It means My God, My God, why have you forsaken me. Do you know what that means?" Sandy again shook her head. The word *forsaken* was not in her vocabulary.

Her uncle looked puzzled, trying to find common ground to explain his words. "Well, it sort of means, 'Daddy, Daddy, why did you leave me?'" *Bam!* All of a sudden, Sandy knew exactly how that man felt. He felt exactly how she had felt when her daddy left her. She wanted that man in her life. She didn't tell anyone.

She went to church on Good Friday and on Palm Sunday with the Preacher and his family and listened very carefully about this Jesus, who understood how it felt for His Daddy to leave Him. Sandy told no one but her best friend what had happened to her.

They were both in sixth grade. Sandy's friend was a Christian, and Sandy confided in her that she believed in Jesus, too. Sandy's friend said she had been born again. This made no sense to Sandy, but this was her very best friend, she just believed what she said. Sandy felt different but couldn't exactly say why.

The Preacher and his family were very poor. He had three children younger than Sandy. The Preacher and his wife decided because she was the oldest, she would get new Easter clothing. On April 21, 1957, Sandy went to church in a mint-green, dotted Swiss dress and new white sandals. That day they had a baptizing in the river. At the end of the baptizing, the Preacher asked, "Is there anyone else who believes in Jesus and wants to be baptized?"

Bam! There went that heart thing again. She didn't even second-guess her feelings, her dress, her shoes, or others' opinion. She waded into the water—mint-green, dotted Swiss dress, white sandals and all! Some words were spoken, and some questions were asked, all of which Sandy could not remember. What she did remember was childlike, but she never forgot the feelings that went with the memories.

The Preacher put her under the water, and she came up shouting. What she said she honestly could not remember, but a feeling passed over her that she had never felt before. Her body was very warm. It felt as if light was streaming out of every pore of her body, and at that time, she didn't even know what a pore was. She honestly did not understand what happened to her, but it had changed her for life. She knew even at that young age she could not make up what happened because she didn't have enough information about Christianity to do that.

According to Jesus's words, her spirit was birthed that day. No one, not even theological scholars, can explain exactly how it happens.

> Flesh gives birth to flesh, but the Spirit gives
> birth to spirit. You should not be surprised at my
> saying, "You must be born again." The wind blows
> wherever it pleases. You hear its sound, but you
> cannot tell where it comes from or where it is going.
> So it is with everyone born of the Spirit. (John
> 3:6–8 NKJV)

I will continue my salvation growth, but I will switch to the first-person tense. Things somehow got very real and personal after my salvation. I was still a child, but I was beginning to understand just how deeply God can impact a life. I felt the Holy Spirit from the time I came up out of the water of baptism, and I know He has never left me.

I was saved, I was baptized, and I was born again! I had Jesus to understand what no one else could. I was listening every time I went to church to see what I had just done and who I had just trusted my life to. But I still had a burning question in my heart: *Daddy, Daddy, why did you leave me?*

There was a building called the Y that during the week was a gas station, small bar, a dance floor, and a jukebox. On Saturday nights, it became the hangout for all the kids in the neighborhood. The bar area was closed. Only Cokes and peanuts were sold. The jukebox had many nickels shoved into it. The kids listened to the latest tunes and danced and danced.

The best part was the Y was about a mile from the small town I lived in, and as the kids walked in groups, there was time to talk and spark with your latest interest. The Preacher was strict in the rules he set but very lenient and loving in his treatment of me. He was adamant about not going to the Y! I could not understand this. I groveled and pleaded with him to let me go every Saturday night.

As I whined one of those nights as, the Preacher said, "Sandy, no daughter of mine will be seen in a beer joint!" *Bam!* There went that heart thing again. I don't remember another word though the lecture was long. I had warm, fuzzy feelings in my heart. His statement reverberated in my being. "No daughter of mine." You could not have dragged me to the Y with grappling hooks after that statement.

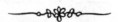

After that, He poured water into a basin and began to wash His disciples' feet, drying them with the towel that was wrapped around Him. Jesus said, "Now that I, your Lord and Teacher, have washed your feet, you also should wash one another's feet. I have set you an example that you should do as I have done for you." (John 13:5, 14, 15 NIV)

The church was going to have a "foot washing," whatever that was. The Preacher lined the women in chairs along the wall on one side and the men along the wall on the other. The Preacher explained that because Jesus was willing to wash the feet of His disciples, we Christians should follow His example and be willing to humble ourselves and do the work of a servant for our brothers and sisters in the Lord.

There was another word I didn't understand, *humble*. I decided it must mean to hunch down so you could reach their feet. I didn't care. If Jesus said it, I was willing to do it. He was my hero!

My turn came, and the woman whose feet I was to wash was the mother of my thirteen-year-old male friend. She had seven children from age one to thirteen. I hunched down in front of her, and she put her feet in the basin. The second my knees hit the floor, *bam*, that heart thing happened again. I felt really little. Not young. Not short. Little.

I took the cloth and began to wash her feet. I realized her feet were rough and worn, and I felt sorry for them. When my hands touched her bare feet, it felt like I had somehow joined with her. I can't explain it but to say I felt like we joined.

I looked up into her face because she had said, "Bless her heart, Lord, bless her little heart." I noticed her eyes were soft, and though I had never thought her to be a beautiful woman, at this time I thought her to be the most beautiful woman in the world.

That was the first foot washing I had ever been to. I'm thinking our churches could use a lot of this "hunching down" activity. It just might make us feel joined to our brothers and sisters. It just might make our brothers and sisters beautiful to us, and it just might bless our hearts.

And, behold, a woman, which was diseased with
an issue of blood twelve years, came behind him,
and touched the hem of his garment. (Matthew
9:20 KJV)

It was inevitable. I was twelve. My "issue of blood" came. I felt like I had a disease. I felt totally ugly. I felt totally changed. Before my "issue," I was quite the tomboy. I played baseball with the guys. I climbed trees. I caught snakes in the swamp to prove my bravery. I could spit, and I even tried "chewing" once!

I told my thirteen-year-old male friend, the one whose mom's feet I washed, to give me a "chaw." He laughed and tore off a hunk. He failed to tell me that after all the spitting and chewing, you threw out the tobacco. I swallowed it! I turned a pale shade of green around the mouth. God has an immense sense of humor and is totally practical. I never much wanted or desired tobacco in any form from that day forward. Thank you, Father God.

With this new thing in life that proved to me beyond the shadow of a doubt I was never going to be one of the guys again, came the responsibility for my foster parents to explain what had happened to my body. The preacher's wife was uncomfortable talking about such things, so the responsibility fell to the Preacher. He was straightforward. He explained the biological aspects of the occurrence. That was the easy part. Next, he started trying to explain the emotional aspects of womanhood. A little stammering occurred here.

He stressed to me how pretty I was. He told me what boys expected from girls and what Jesus expected from girls. He told me never to give in to what the boys wanted. I should always do what I thought

Jesus would want me to do even if my feelings told me different. No problem. Jesus was my hero. Little did I realize what a challenge this would be for my female feelings as I became older.

You might not think it was too big a responsibility to tell a twelve-year-old girl the facts of life, him being a Preacher and all. Looking back, I know it was a big deal. You see, the Preacher was only twenty-eight years old, and his wife was only twenty-three. What a job for two young people.

Don't ever think foster care doesn't work. Foster care was instrumental in saving my baseball-playing, tree-climbing, snake-catching, spitting, chewing, tomboy soul!

Above all, love each other deeply, because love
covers over a multitude of sins. (1 Peter 4:7–8 NIV)

One day in the summer of the twelfth year of my life, not too long after my salvation, my so-called friends began to taunt me. They teased me, saying my mom was never going to return for me. They told me I probably didn't even have two sisters like I had said. Being twelve and sensitive to peer pressure, I lied.

I said, "That's all you know! The Preacher is going to take me to see my baby sister this weekend." They all got very quiet. *There,* I thought, *I put them in their places!* I turned to walk away in anger and looked smack into the face of the Preacher. My face flamed with embarrassment because of the lie. What was he going to think? What was he going to say to me?

He was quiet for what I thought was an eternity and then he spoke. "Sandy, you better go get packed. We will be leaving pretty soon." *Bam!* There's that heart thing again.

I don't know how he filled the pulpit that week. I don't know where he got the money to take me. I don't know how his old car made it the three hundred miles to where my baby sister was. I just know that on that day, his love covered not only my sin but saved my lying little face. He never mentioned the incident again, but the lesson it taught me is still with me.

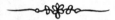

Pure and genuine religion in the sight of God the Father means caring for orphans and widows in their distress and refusing to let the world corrupt you. (James 1:27 NLT)

My friends continued to tell me Mom would never return for me. They were wrong. In the fall of August of 1957, she came from Detroit, Michigan, where she had been remanded into the custody of her brother, to pick me up. She had proven she could be a responsible adult by holding down a job and procuring living quarters for her three children.

As I got ready to leave the Preacher's home, he spoke to my mom in private. I later found out he saved all the money he received for my foster care and gave it to her to help her get a fresh start.

As I was leaving, I hugged the Preacher and saw a look on his face I could not quite understand. I had never noticed it before. It was human adult sadness. It was pain. *Bam!* My heart hurt. Being a kid and very excited and very selfish, I forgot about it for many years, until I looked him up and questioned him about that time in his life. In retrospect, I realize the Preacher was living James 1:27 (NLT) at that time.

On a theological note, I know in my heart that verse goes much deeper. An orphan is someone who has no parents. We are all spiritual orphans until God the Father adopts us. A widow is someone who has no husband. Jesus Christ died so He could become our husband; we are His brides.

Pure and genuine religion in the sight of God the Father means caring for spiritual orphans by guiding them to the Father in heaven.

Pure and genuine religion in the sight of God the Father means caring for spiritual widows in their distress of not having husbands by guiding them to Jesus Christ. Pure and genuine religion in the sight of God the Father means refusing to let the world corrupt you.

It is strange when people ask what my salvation verse was and I have to tell them.

> About the ninth hour Jesus cried out in a loud
> voice, "Eloi, Eloi, lama sabachthani?" which means,
> "My God, my God, why have You forsaken Me?"
> (Matthew 27:46 NKJV)

As a twelve-year-old child, all I knew how to do was picture the face of that man on the cross. How sad He must have looked because His Daddy left Him. I loved Him so much my insides burned with understanding. I wanted to tell everyone around me what He had done for me. He knew how I felt. No one else in the world had ever known how I felt. I wanted to take the few words I knew about Him and spread them all around for the whole world to see how great He was to me.

I have never grown out of that childlike expectation and love of Jesus. He is still my hero. I am still His little girl. My greatest hope is that He will return soon and take me to be with Him forever. This is why I sign everything "Maranatha." It is of Aramaic origin and means "Our Lord has come." Indeed, He came the first time and will return again to take me to be with Him forever!

This is why I write: A writer has the gift of words. A writer is a word missionary.

PARABLES

All these things spake Jesus to the multitude in
parables; and without a parable spake He not unto
them.

Matthew 13:34 KJV

A parable, by the definition I use, is a common-day incident with a
spiritual application. The Lord Jesus has given me the heart of a very
simple person to see His teachings in many everyday occurrences.

For this I am very thankful. I have to admit, being a storyteller,
I love it when the Lord Jesus gives me a spiritual application in an
everyday happening.

The following "Mom parables," as I have referred to them all my
life, are what I have received from my Lord and Savior in whatever
aspect of life or living I find myself.

Hide-and-Seek

Listen to my prayer, O God. And do not hide
Yourself from my pleading.
—Psalm 55:1 (NIV)

In the early years of my marriage, my young daughter, Ruth Elaine, played hide-and-seek with her daddy in our small, four-room apartment. They loved that game! I don't know who got the greater pleasure, Ruthie or my husband, Sam.

When Ruthie found her daddy, she shouted and laughed with glee. Sam would throw her into the air, laugh, and say, "You found me. You found me."

Sam constantly tried to find new places to hide. This was not easy to do. One day he went into the hallway and climbed up the wall like Spider-Man. He inched his way up to the ceiling, one arm and leg on each side of the hall, and softly called, "Ruthie, come and find me."

She heard the voice but could not find her daddy in all the old, familiar places. She became discouraged. Her daddy said a bit louder, "Ruthie, come and find me. Here I am." She went toward the voice, but her senses kept her from looking up. She was very near tears, so he said a bit louder, "Ruthie, Ruthie, come and find me. I'm *up* here."

She was obedient to her daddy. Rather than running toward the voice only, she listened to the directions. She looked up! Out came a shout of glee from her. "I found you; I found you!"

Sam dropped to her level and picked her up. He threw her into the air. "You found me; you found me!"

I am sometimes like little Ruthie. I feel like God is hiding from me, so I look in familiar places. I read the Word, I pray, I sing; but I don't hear His voice calling. I'm trusting my senses. I begin to get discouraged and pout and cry. Ah, but Daddy loves me. He calls a little louder, "I am up here!"

Finally, I listen to His direction and look up. Sure enough, there He is! My heart and soul shout with glee, "I found You; I found You!"

He drops to my level. He picks me up out of my despair, throws me heavenward, and shouts with pleasure, "You found Me; you found Me."

I don't know who gets the greater pleasure, my Father God or me!

Thank You, God, for seeking and finding me.
Amen.

Snares and Rings

Our soul is escaped as a bird out of the snare of the
fowlers: the snare is broken, and we are escaped.
Our help is in the name of the Lord, who made
heaven and earth.

—Psalm 24:7–8 (KJV)

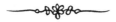

I have a beautiful daughter named Laura Beth, who was born with a congenital defect. She was born with her right arm missing from about three inches below the shoulder. This has never stopped her from living a very normal life, but it did get her into trouble when she was about four years old.

Her dad was a student at Wayne State University in Detroit, Michigan. He had a three-ring notebook filled with lecture notes that had to be handed in at the end of the semester. If he didn't hand it in, he failed the course.

The problem was that Laura loved to snap that notebook open and closed. She liked the snapping sound. Her dad told me not to let Laura get ahold of that notebook because he was fearful she'd destroy his precious lecture notes. I gave the appropriate rules to my little daughter, stressing that if she touched the notebook, she would be spanked. I went about my normal day.

I was at the sink, washing dishes, when I heard *snap!* I am not a very good disciplinarian, so I didn't want to hear that sound. I thought, *She'll put it away, and I might not have to spank her.*

Suddenly, I heard very quiet but very discernible weeping. I silently went around the corner and discovered Laura's hand was caught between the rings of the notebook, and they were cutting into her hand. She had no way to free herself.

I quickly removed her hand, held her, and asked, "Why didn't you call me to come and help you?"

She said, "I knew I wasn't supposed to play with Dad's notebook, and I was afraid to call you."

My heart broke. Now I had to mete out the spanking I had promised. I didn't want to. I felt the pain of the rings biting into her hand was probably enough. But I am a parent, and consistency is very important. I explained the punishment, gave her a halfhearted smack on the bottom, hugged her, and sent her on her way. That spanking hurt me more than it could have ever hurt her.

How like Laura we are sometimes. We disobey our Father. We get hurt by sin. We weep and cry. We don't call out to Him to come and free us from the sin we are in because we are afraid of Him. He hears us weeping and comes and frees us from the sin. Then, just like a parent, He has to mete out the spanking because He is holy and must be obeyed. He forgives us. He holds us on His ample lap and consoles us. The chastisement hurts Him every bit as much as it hurts us.

Thank You, Lord, for chastising me because You
love me as Your own child. Amen.

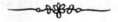

No Santa

But you must remain faithful to the things you
have been taught. You know they are true, for you
know you can trust those who taught you. You have
been taught the holy Scriptures from childhood,
and they have given you the wisdom to receive the
salvation that comes by trusting in Christ Jesus.

—2 Timothy 3:14–15

When my children were younger, my husband and I decided not to teach them there was a Santa. I got a lot of flak from other family members, but I stuck to my guns. One year, my second daughter, Laura, was watching the news on TV, and the announcers said they saw a strange sight on radar. They had superimposed Santa and his reindeer on the weather map.

Laura wanted to know if there were no Santa, why adults on TV were lying for all the people to see. Surely there must be a Santa. It was a rough moment. Had we made the wrong choice? Had we stolen her childhood away?

I told her Santa was a game, and many families played it. She said, "But the moms and dads aren't telling the truth to their kids!" I told her that her dad and I would not lie to her about Santa or other things.

Years later, when it came time for her to make the decision to believe in God, whom she could not see, I hoped she remembered her dad and I didn't lie to her about Santa or God.

By the way, Christmas is her favorite holiday. You have never seen a house so decked out for Christmas. You have never seen someone really enjoy the holidays until you see my daughter's remembrance of her Lord and Savior's birth!

Thank You, Lord, for being my truth and requiring
Your truth in my life. Amen.

The Helmet

And take the helmet of salvation, and the sword
of the Spirit, which is the word of God: Praying
always with all prayer and supplication in the Spirit,
and watching thereunto with all perseverance and
supplication for all saints.

—Ephesians 6:17–18 (KJV)

Laura had very long, black hair as a child. I sat on our front porch and brushed her beautiful hair on spring mornings. I cleaned the brush and threw away the hair. What I thought to be trash, a very persistent blue jay, an extremely cruel and heartless bird, thought was building treasure. The nest was being built and prepared for the laying of eggs.

This created a problem. The morning gleanings from the brush were not quite enough to finish the nest as quickly as the bird desired. That bird dive-bombed my little daughter and pecked at her hair to obtain more building material. I called the animal protection league, and they gave advice only: "Have your daughter wear a helmet until nesting season is over in about two weeks."

We have a very wicked and cruel predator that would love to use us for nesting material. His name is Satan. He loves to dive-bomb God's saints and peck at their minds to obtain nesting material to plant his wicked eggs of sin. Our protector has left us a defense: the helmet of salvation! But we must make sure it covers our minds. He left us the Word of God, but we must make sure we read it and get it firmly placed in our thoughts so it will be revealed in our actions. God left us the power of prayer and supplication, but to cover our souls, we must pray and make supplication through the Holy Spirit for ourselves as well as for other Christians.

Are your mind, actions, and soul covered today?

Thank You, Lord, for Your Word in my life. Amen.

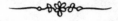

The True Light

That was the true Light, which lighteth every man
that cometh into the world.

—John 1:9 (KJV)

When our daughters were four and six years old we went out West. Daddy took the girls exploring in some caves. He made sure he had a good flashlight, and off they went. At one point in time, he came upon some steps going down deeper into the cave. Not knowing what was ahead, he instructed the girls to sit and wait on the stairs while he went ahead to make sure it was a safe path.

Laura became terrified when she no longer held her daddy's hand, and the light disappeared from her sight. She began to cry. Daddy came back, just as he promised, and with him came the security of a hand held tightly and a light to guide the way.

Do you ever feel that way about your Light, Jesus Christ? You are holding firmly to His hand one moment, and His Light is shining brightly on your path. All of a sudden, you do not feel His hand in yours anymore. The Light has gone from your sight. You begin to cry.

Sometimes God tells us to wait while He goes ahead to make sure our path is clear. Just because you do not feel Him or detect His Light in your life does not mean He has ceased to be with you. Your faith is stretched in this way. If He says, "Sit and wait," then sit and wait. He will come back for you when the way is clear and the path is safe.

Wait on the Lord: be of good courage, and he shall
strengthen thine heart: wait, I say, on the Lord.
(Psalm 27:14 KJV)

Thank You, Lord, for holding me close even when I
do not feel You are there. Thank You for Your Light
even when I cannot see it. Amen.

A Child's Expectation

But when Jesus saw it, he was much displeased, and
said unto them, Suffer the little children to come
unto me, and forbid them not: for of such is the
kingdom of God. Verily I say unto you, Whosoever
shall not receive the kingdom of God as a little
child, he shall not enter therein.

—Mark 10:14–15 (KJV)

Even so, come, Lord Jesus.

—Revelation 22:20 (KJV)

When my youngest daughter, Cristi Ana, was about four years old,
she had an insatiable desire to know about Jesus. She kept telling
me she wanted to go see Him. She wanted to ask Him how he made
dandelions. She wanted to know how He made seagulls, frogs, and
worms. She wanted to ask Him why vegetable seeds, despite being so
tiny, could make big vegetables.

One day after a seeming 1,001 questions about Jesus, almost in
frustration I told her, "Cristi, to go see Jesus we have to die first." Here
big, blue-green eyes opened very wide, and she got strangely quiet.

About two hours later, as I was attempting to get some work
done, she came running up to me all excited. Her conversation went
something like this. "Mom, I know what will happen. We are going
to see Jesus. You and me are going to be in the car, and we are going
to have an accident. A big angel will come and take you by the hand,
a little angel will come and take me by the hand, and we will go see
Jesus!"

You can imagine how I must have felt. Did my daughter have some inside information from Jesus that I did not know? Every time I got into the car alone with Cristi and went anywhere, I wondered if her words would come true!

Finally, a few days later, curiosity caused me to ask her, "Cristi, why did you tell me we were going to have a car accident?"

Her excited, four-year-old voice piped up, "Well, Mom, you said we couldn't go see Jesus unless we died. I didn't want to go to heaven and leave you alone, so I thought if we had a car accident, we could go together. And Mom, I really want to see Jesus!"

What a lesson for Mom. Now I know why Jesus said the kingdom of heaven is filled with this kind of expectation—childlike expectation that Jesus will come and take us home at any given moment. I sometimes get so bogged down living this life I forget to realize this life is a dim shadow of what great expectations await us in heaven.

Through this daughter of mine, I have succeeded in keeping my childlike expectation of the coming of my Lord. This is one of the reasons I always sign off "Maranatha." It means "the Lord is coming." Let me live it in the innocence and expectation of a child, the child of God I am!

And Cristi? She spent two years in Africa with Wycliffe Bible Translators as a short-term missionary. She is married now but will be a kid at heart for the rest of her life. She has never lost that childlike expectation for her Jesus. It rubs off on anyone who knows her.

Even so, come, Lord Jesus!

Thank You, Lord, for the childlike expectation of
Your coming back for me. Amen.

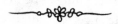

Jesus Goes to Georgia

Then he said to Him, "If Your Presence does not go
with us, do not bring us up from here.
—Exodus 33:14–15 (NKJV)

I had a friend who lived in Georgia. She was going through some
rough times, and I felt an urge to visit her and encourage her in some
way. I had a problem. I was the mother of three active children and
the office manager of my husband's small business. I felt guilty about
leaving my family and responsibilities behind in my need to visit a
friend.

My husband encouraged me to go and not let guilt keep me from
doing what I felt God wanted me to do. So with a measure of guilt and
some apprehension about leaving my two older children alone with
Dad, I made my plans for the two-day drive.

Cristi was four years old, and it was decided she would go with
me. I was up before dawn and loaded the car. I made a small bed on
the backseat for my daughter and tucked her in to sleep for a few hours
more.

Guilt made me sit for a while and ponder my decision. I began to
pray softly. From the backseat a small head popped up and a childish
voice asked, "Who you talking to?"

"I was talking to Jesus."

The same childlike voice piped up, "Is He going to Georgia
with us?"

I realized then and there how wrong my fears were. God is
omnipresent and would take care of my family in Ohio. He indeed
would take care of my daughter and me as we went to Georgia in

obedience to Him. I answered my little girl, "Yes, Cristi, Jesus is going to Georgia with us." And He did.

> Lord, thank You for words of wisdom from the innocent mouth of a child. Your presence goes with us wherever we go in obedience to You. Please don't let guilt or apprehension keep me from doing Your will. Amen.

God, You're My Boy!

At the same time came the disciples unto Jesus,
saying, Who is the greatest in the kingdom of
heaven? And Jesus called a little child unto him,
and set him in the midst of them, And said, Verily
I say unto you, Except ye be converted, and
become as little children, ye shall not enter into the
kingdom of heaven.

—Matthew 18:1–3 (KJV)

After eighteen years and three daughters, I finally had a son, Samuel. I would pick him up, hug him to myself, and say, "I love you. You're my boy."

He came to associate these words of love and affirmation in a completely childlike understanding. He had no idea at age three the difference between a girl and a boy. He didn't have a concept of what "boy" meant. He just knew I held him, hugged him, and speak those special words: "I love you. You're my boy."

One day he was feeling especially tender toward me. He wanted to let me know this. He ran up to me, wrapped his tiny arms around my legs, looked up into my face, and said with all the gusto of a three-year-old, "Mommy, I love you. You're my boy!"

I felt like a million dollars. Never had I experienced such a beautiful outpouring of love from someone with such an incorrect grouping of words. I totally understood his meaning. It made my day.

This is a good lesson for all us so-called mature Christians. We watch new converts to the Lord. They pray with gusto in a childlike manner. They don't exactly get Scripture correct all the time. They are emotional and spontaneous. We might get the urge to correct them. Why?

The Lord understands their hearts. Their actions might be an outpouring of love through a collection of incorrect words we don't really agree with or understand, but guess what? The Lord totally understands the intentions of their hearts and totally understands what they mean.

I bet He hears, "God, I love You. You're my boy." I bet it makes His day!

Thank You, Lord, for my simple childlike
expectations of Your return for me. Amen.

Seek His Face

Seek the Lord, and his strength: seek his face
evermore.

—Psalm 105:4 (NIV)

The Lord turned and looked straight at Peter. Then
Peter remembered the word the Lord had spoken
to him: "Before the rooster crows today, you will
disown me three times." And he went outside and
wept bitterly.

—Luke 22:61 (NIV)

When my son, Samuel, was very young, he learned something that is a prevailing trait of mine. When I talk to you, I look you straight in the eyes. My children know that if I looked straight into their eyes, they had my utmost attention.

One day Samuel was prattling on and on in his childish way, and I was trying to do other things. He said, "Mom, you're not listening to me!"

In frustration, I replied, "Samuel, I'm listening!"

He calmly said to me, "But Mom, your eyes aren't listening."

The Lord is not a human mom; He is a spiritual one. He looks you straight in the face and listens to what you have to say. In the verse taken from Psalm, "seek His face" is a Hebrew saying for worship and prayer. There are no sin barriers between you and God. Look Him straight in the eyes and speak to Him in worship and prayer. What a blessing!

What if your life was not pure before Him? What if you denied Him in your life and actions? What if you avoid the eyes of Jesus because you failed Him? It is then He will gently turn you around and peer into your face and heart. The knowledge of your sin will burn, and you will remember the Word of the Lord He has spoken to you in your life. You will weep bitter tears, but you will be restored to the Lord and again have sweet fellowship with your Lord, just as Peter did.

Remember: it is the Lord's strength He asks you to rely on, not your own. Do your part, and seek His face in prayer and worship. He will do the rest for you.

> Help me, Lord, to always seek Your face and not my
> own selfish desires and ambitions. Amen.

Toys in Heaven

However, as it is written: "No eye has seen, no ear
has heard, no mind has conceived what God has
prepared for those who love him."

—1 Corinthians 2:9 (NIV)

When Samuel was five years old, he drove me crazy with a habit he had. No matter where we were going, he frantically looked for the perfect toy to stick in his pocket before leaving the house.

After trying to cope with this oddity in my little son, I finally got frustrated. I asked him one day while waiting rather impatiently for him to find that "perfect toy," "Samuel, why in the world do you always have to have a toy in your pocket all the time?"

He looked at me with those big, beautiful, dark eyes and answered quite innocently, in the voice of a trusting child, "Because of what you said, Mom."

Now that was a shocker! What had I said to make Samuel interpret the need to have a toy in his pocket all the time? "When did I ever tell you that you must have a toy in your pocket all the time?"

"Well, remember when I asked you if there is going to be toys in heaven? Well, you said to me we won't need toys in heaven. Jesus will be all we need. You said Jesus might come and take us anytime. What if He comes when we are out? I know you are right, so when He comes, I want to be ready. I want toys in heaven!"

Lord Jesus, my son was listening and believing everything I told him about You. Thank You, Lord! How thankful I am that our home was one that could nourish a belief and certainty of You returning to take us to heaven. Amen.

Bad Actions, Good Intentions

Then hear thou in heaven thy dwelling place, and forgive, and do, and give to every man according to his ways, whose heart thou knowest; for thou, even thou only, knowest the hearts of all the children of men.

—1 Kings 8:39 (KJV)

For the word of God is quick, and powerful, and sharper than any two-edged sword, piercing even to the dividing asunder of soul and spirit, and of the joints and marrow, and is a discerner of the thoughts and intents of the heart.

—Hebrews 4:12 (KJV)

When my son was a first-grader at a Christian school, he received a paddling from the principal. He had broken the no fighting rule. He was on the playground at recess, and the fourth-grade bully hit his little brother, Andre, and took the swing away from him. Samuel rushed in, very protectively, and knocked the bully to the ground, giving him a few deserved punches.

Samuel and I were called into the principal's office, and I had to watch as the punishment was inflicted. Samuel was stone quiet and took the paddle with courage. I then had to escort him back to class. It was during this time I condoned my son's intentions.

I asked him if he understood he had to have a paddling because he had broken a school rule. He said, "Yes, but that boy was wrong, He's always pushing people around, and all the kids are afraid of him. He hit Andre, and I got mad!"

I told him I was proud of him for standing up for what was right. I told him I knew where his heart was. I told him he should never stand by and watch as other people were treated wrongly.

Now the tears came. I hugged him really close and told him I was proud of him. I said, "I'm not proud because you broke a rule. I'm proud because you stood up for your brother."

I wondered if I had done the right thing condoning Samuel for an action contrary to school rules. Then the Lord Jesus graciously let me remember two stories.

I remembered when the midwives of the Hebrew women would not kill the Hebrew babies as the Egyptian authorities had commanded. This action, contrary to government rules, saved lives! It saved the life of Moses, the leader of the Hebrew nation. God condoned their actions.

> I remembered Rahab, who hid Hebrew spies from
> her government. She secretly housed the two spies
> Joshua sent to explore Jericho and helped them
> escape by hiding them in stalks of flax on her roof.
> Rahab sent the king's messengers on a false trail.
> Then Rahab let the two spies down the outside
> wall, using a rope through the window of her house.
> Later, she lied to the officials, saying, "Yes, the men
> came to me, but I did not know where they had
> come from. At dusk, when it was time to close the
> city gate, the men left. I don't know which way they
> went. Go after them quickly. You may catch up with
> them."
> —Joshua 2:4-5 (NIV)

Samuel broke a rule. His actions were wrong. The midwives broke a law; they're actions were wrong. Rahab lied and harbored enemies; her actions were wrong. God does not always judge wrong actions.

God sees into the heart and judges its intentions. Humankind will always stick to the letter of the law because they cannot read hearts. God Almighty judges the intentions of your heart.

Dear Lord, may my actions be honoring to You, and may my intentions be pure in Your sight. Amen.

Blessings and Babies

My frame was not hidden from you when I was
made in the secret place. When I was woven
together in the womb, your eyes saw my unformed
body. All the days ordained for me were written in
your book before one of them came to be.
—Psalm 139:15–16 (NIV)

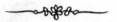

My last child, Andre Jonathan, is a witty, gentle, obedient, and compliant child. He is the laughter and joy of my life. When he was a teenager in high school, he was on a debate team in home and family living. He took the prolife stance. The other team took the pro-choice stance. The teacher was definitely pro-choice, and this made Andre's side almost destined to lose. He asked my advice. Being a storyteller, I told him a story.

"Andre, what advice would you give a mother who was in very poor health and had a baby that could have killed her? She became pregnant yet again, and the little boy died five and a half months in the womb from her health problems or from a malformation in the womb; the reason was never determined. She gets pregnant yet again and has a child with handicaps.

"She gets pregnant yet again, and the child dies in the womb at six weeks. Yet again she gets pregnant, and the child is born and given a maximum of three years to live. The mother has an operation to help her carry her babies and gets pregnant again. She has a healthy baby, but by this time, she is getting too old to have more children.

"She becomes pregnant in her midlife, and the medical profession advises that she abort the child. It is too dangerous for her health to carry it full term. With the history of her past pregnancies, there is a good possibility the baby will be deformed or die in the womb. She is too old to have a child safely as the odds of having a baby with Down's syndrome are great at her age. What would you advise the mother, Andre?"

Andre looked me straight in the eyes and said, "I would tell that mother to have that baby, and let God take care of whatever happens."

"That's exactly what I did, and that's why you are here today. I am that mother, and you are that baby. Go tell that to your classmates!"

He did, and his team won! Andre is married now and has children of his own. They are perfectly healthy and being taught about the Lord.

Lord Jesus, think of the joys and blessings we lose
from not trusting You in the areas of our unborn
children. Amen.

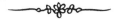

The Splinter

And why look at the splinter in your brother's
eye, but don't consider the beam that is in your
own eye?

—Luke 6:41 (NLT)

Samuel was enjoying the warmth of a fresh spring day. He ran to me
and asked if he could take off his shoes. He loved to run and play
barefoot. I couldn't resist the pleading look on his face. *It can't hurt,*
I thought.

Off came the shoes! Off came the socks! Away went Samuel to
romp and play unhindered. He frolicked in the yard and bragged to
the other children whose mothers would not allow them to take off
their shoes. I enjoyed the music of my son's laughter as I sat reading a
book on the porch swing.

Samuel soon limped up the porch steps, looking apprehensive.
He told me his foot hurt. I looked and saw an ugly splinter protruding
from between his big toe and the adjacent toe. I knew the splinter had
to come out, or it could cause more pain and possible infection.

I began to reason with Samuel. I told him if the splinter was
not removed, it would cause more pain. Although he did not totally
understand, he agreed to let me remove it. I took a pair of tweezers
and pulled the splinter out of that tender little foot.

It did indeed hurt, but Samuel trusted me. He cried, and I consoled
him as he sat on my lap. I let him know I was so proud of him for being
brave. I told him it could have been much worse if he hadn't told me
about the splinter and I hadn't taken it out. Samuel thanked me for
removing the splinter. He wiped the tears from his eyes and gave me

a quick hug. Off he ran, still barefoot, to play with his friends. He was a happy little boy again.

I returned to my book. Just as I was getting deep into the plot, Samuel limped up to the porch swing, looking very frightened. "Mom it still hurts deep inside," he whined. I looked at his foot and realized part of the splinter was still there. My heart started to pound. I knew the pain I must inflict on my son to remove the broken splinter from beneath the surface. I dreaded what I knew I must do.

Now I had to tell my trusting little boy the entire splinter hadn't come out; I had to remove the broken piece from below the surface. He asked if it would hurt. I was honest and said it would hurt very much. He cried. I held him close and cried with him.

I told him to sit on the swing while I went in to sterilize a needle. Samuel sat forlorn and scared. I almost decided to take him to the doctor instead of attempting this alone. Samuel was afraid of doctors and felt more comfortable with me, so I decided to go ahead and remove the splinter myself. It wouldn't hurt any less, but at least someone who loved him would cause the pain. This was comfort of a small sort to Samuel.

I told Samuel to sit as still as he could. If he squirmed, it might cause me to poke his foot in the wrong place. Then I would just have to poke and hurt him all over again. He looked up with fearful yet trusting eyes. That simple look melted my heart.

I began to squeeze and pinch to locate the splinter. It was very deep below the surface, and I knew it would hurt very much when I pried it out. Samuel sat as still as he could, considering the pain he was experiencing, but he cried and cried. I rubbed my eyes repeatedly to see what I was doing because I cried with him. Samuel looked up at me and suddenly sat very still. I realized he was gritting his teeth against the pain so I wouldn't cry anymore.

Finally, the ugly splinter worked up to the surface of the flesh. I pulled it out very slowly so it wouldn't break again. I showed the splinter to Samuel. We both talked about how ugly it was and all the trouble it caused. I wiped away Samuel's tears and gave him a hug. He hugged me back with all his little boy strength. He thanked me yet again for taking the ugly splinter out. I knew I had finally gotten the entire splinter. It wouldn't cause Samuel more pain.

How like Samuel I am when I come to the Lord. I come with my splinter problem of sin, and He takes it out by forgiving me. I sit on His lap and thank Him for helping me. It really didn't hurt too much after all! I run back out into my life. I am free for the time being.

I soon realize something is wrong. I go back and tell the Lord I still hurt deep inside. He says He has forgiven me, but I am still carrying an ugly sin splinter deep under the surface. He knows it's there and informs me it will hurt very much to remove it. He tells me I have to be purified by His Spirit and have that sin splinter dug out by the roots. I cry out in fear. He holds me and cries with me.

I cry because I am terrified. He waits with patience. Finally, I look up with fearful but trusting eyes, having faith in my Lord. He tells me how important it is for me to cooperate with Him. The more I resist, the more He has to prod me. I sit as still as I can considering the pain, but I sob in agony. I grit my teeth and look into His face, knowing I don't want to hurt Him. Yet I want to be rid of that painful sin splinter in my life. Finally, I sit very still.

The sin splinter is worked up to the surface of my flesh, and the Lord pulls it out very carefully, root and all, and we both cry. He holds me close and consoles me. I tell Him how thankful I am He has removed the sin splinter totally. His love calms and soothes me. He wipes away my tears, and I watch Him also wipe away His. I climb off His lap and run on in my childish way. I am free and whole for yet another day.

Thank You, Father God, for removing my sin
splinters and making me whole again. Amen.

The Gate Home

But made Himself of no reputation, and took upon
Him the form of a servant, and was made in the
likeness of men.
    —Philippians 2:7 (NIV)

I am the gate; whoever enters through me will be
saved.
    —John 10:8–9 (NIV)

We live very close to a park with a forest behind. Deer often venture
into our neighborhood. On one such occasion, a young deer was
separated from its mother and wandered into our neighbor's backyard.
He became frightened when he found himself in a fenced-in area with
no seeming way of escape.

My son Samuel and his friend Victor decided to help the small
deer back to its home in the forest. The deer was terrified of them.
Every time they approached the deer to show it the gate out of the
backyard, it panicked and crashed against the fence. The deer did
not understand they were trying to help him by showing it the gate
to freedom.

They tried and tried and tried. The more they tried, the more
frightened the deer became. It bled from its wounds. Samuel was in
tears. He asked me, "Why doesn't it know we want to help it? Look at
the deer. It's hurt and afraid of us, and all we want to do is help it! It
can't find the gate to get out. Why won't it just trust us?"

"Samuel, it's afraid of you because it is a deer, and you are human. If you were a deer, it would trust you."

Isn't that the way we are toward God? We are fenced in by sin. Our sins have blinded our eyes to the gate back home to God. All God wants is for us to trust Him. Jesus Christ is the only gate to freedom. God approaches us and tries to help us. We are afraid and try to run away from Him. Life leaves us hurt and bleeding. But He knows. He puts on skin, comes down to us, and gently leads us through the gate and back home.

Thank You, Lord Jesus, for coming down to this
sin-sick world and being my gate back to the Father
in heaven. Amen.

Mud and Miracles

I waited patiently for the Lord; he turned to me and heard my cry. He lifted me out of the slimy pit, out of the mud and mire; he set my feet on a rock and gave me a firm place to stand. He put a new song in my mouth, a hymn of praise to our God. Many will see and fear and put their trust in the Lord.

—Psalm 40:1–3 (NIV)

Victor, Samuel's best friend, had an older brother, Derek. Derek was a drummer in a rock band. He had a full set of black drums Samuel really loved. When he visited Victor, he was not supposed to touch Derek's drums.

One day Samuel did something that really angered Derek. If the truth be known, Samuel probably played Derek's drums! Derek told him he was going to get him and beat him up. He was twice Samuel's size. Samuel commenced running with all his might.

Just like emotional David in the Bible, Samuel began to call on the Lord! But he wasn't very patient; he didn't have a whole lot of time. Samuel ran with all his adrenaline-powered energy. He knew Derek would still catch him if something didn't happen and happen fast. Samuel's prayer went something like this: "Lord, if you let me get away from Derek, I promise I will never bug him again. Please, Lord, help me!"

It had rained that day, and the rain left a small patch of mud on the firm sidewalk. Samuel saw it, jumped clean over it, and kept on trucking. Derek didn't see the mud. He slipped and fell. This gave Samuel just enough lead time to get home, slam the door, lock it, and come running to me for protection. Samuel told me how the Lord saved him with a miracle.

> Lord, I get myself in all kinds of trouble by my own
> foolishness. I ask You to get me out of trouble. I cry!
> You reach down, plant my feet on the solid rock,
> and give me a firm place to stand. Help this put a
> song in my mouth and hymns of praises to You,
> God. Amen.

His Hand Is Secure

I give them eternal life, and they shall never perish;
no one can snatch them out of my hand.
—John 10:28 (NIV)

My heart has been engrossed in the Lord's hands. I see how difficult it is to stay patiently in the grasp of the Lord and not squirm to do my own thing. I don't always succeed.

I thought of yet another story about Samuel at age four. As we took a walk, he kept trying to let go of my hand so he could forge ahead on his own. I was afraid he would get hurt, so I grasped his hand tighter and tighter until he called out, "Ouch, you're hurting me!"

I countered, "Samuel, I'm not hurting you. You are hurting you. Quit struggling."

It has been that way with me lately. The Lord is holding tighter and tighter, and I cry out, "Ouch, you're hurting me." He gently reminds me to quit struggling. It is I causing the pain by trying to escape His great love. He sees my future and He loves me. He will never let me go.

Do you feel the hand of the Lord holding you tighter and tighter? He will never let you go. Quit struggling. The Lord holds on to you, and He will never let you go. This should produce great comfort in your heart and life.

Lord, forgive me when I struggle to have my own way. It is my struggling that causes my pain. Help me to rest calmly and trustingly in the palm of Your omnipotent hand. Amen.

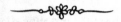

Heavenly Road Map

Nevertheless I am continually with You; You hold
me by my right hand.
—Psalm 73:23 (NKJV)

I was walking through a shopping mall with my grandson, Nathan. He was three years old at the time. I was having a difficult time persuading him to hold my hand so he wouldn't get separated from us. I hit on what I thought was a good idea. I told him, "Nathan, will you hold my hand so I won't get lost?" It worked! He clung tightly to my hand so "Grama" wouldn't get lost.

I wonder if our heavenly Father feels this way about us. We are always running ahead of Him and getting into things we shouldn't. Does He get impatient, or does He just cling tighter to our hand? We are little children to God and must stay with Him continually or get lost.

I marvel that sometimes we get self-sufficient and think we are leading God by the hand to make sure He doesn't get lost. We think we know best where we should go, yet God has another itinerary for our lives. We better hold on to the hand of the One who is the Father, and let Him take us where we need to be. He knows the heavenly road map of your life.

Dear heavenly Father, thank You for your patience
with my attempt at self-sufficiency. There is no such
thing, yet at times I forge ahead and get lost from
You. Thank You for coming and reminding me You
are never lost from me. Amen.

Hold My Hand, Precious Lord

Where can I go from Your Spirit? Or where can I
flee from Your presence? ... Even there your hand
shall lead me, and Your right hand shall hold me.
—Psalm 139:7, 10 (NKJV)

My younger sister wanted to cross the street by herself. She had been told she was too young to cross alone and must have someone holding her hand for her safety's sake. She didn't like this rule. She wanted to be independent and cross all alone.

One day in exasperation she said, "I want to cross the street." She was told not right now; someone had to go with her and hold her hand. She grabbed her tiny right hand in her left hand and blurted out in sheer frustration, "I'll hold my own hand!"

How like that tiny girl we are. We want to forge ahead of the Lord and ignore His Spirit and presence. We want to hold our own hands because we don't see the danger of crossing the streets of life alone.

But like the psalmist, we must recognize there is no place in all eternity from which we can escape the Spirit and presence of God. Better let Him hold your hand and guide you across to eternity.

Praise You, Father, for Your strong right hand that
guides and holds me safely in all the areas of this
dangerous, sin-filled world. Amen.

In Jesus

These things I have spoken unto you, that in Me
ye might have peace. In the world ye shall have
tribulation: but be of good cheer; I have overcome
the world.

—John 16:33 (KJV)

I watched as my little grandson ran and played with his uncle. His
uncle chased him, and my grandson ran and jumped in his dad's lap,
hiding his face to feel safe. If he raised his head and his uncle was near,
he hid his face again to feel the peace and safety of his dad's lap.

The Lord Jesus gave us this option. If we feel fear in the world, it is
because we are not sitting on the lap of Jesus (in Jesus), hiding our faces
from the world. The word *peace* in this verse literally means "oneness,
peace, quietness, rest." The word *tribulation* means "afflicted, anguish,
burdened, persecution, troubled."

As Christians we sometimes do not realize we already sit on Jesus's
lap. Ephesians 2:6 (NIV) tells us, "God raised us up with Christ and
seated us with Him in the heavenly realms in Jesus." It's a done deal!

If you look up and see the affliction, anguish, burdens,
persecutions, and troubles of this world, quickly hide yourself in Jesus.
You will immediately feel the oneness, peace, quietness, and rest only
He can give.

You don't have to overcome the world; Jesus already did this for
you. You just have to jump in His lap and hide your face from all that
would harm you. Don't lift your face to any other face except that of

Jesus. "Seek the Lord, and his strength: seek his face evermore (Psalm 105:4 KJV).

> Jesus, what a joy to hide in You. What a peace You
> give me when I hide my face in You. Amen.

Milk Money, and Revenge

For we know Him that hath said, Vengeance
belongeth unto Me, I will recompense, saith the
Lord. And again, The Lord shall judge His people.

—Hebrews 10:30 (KJV)

Younger brother David was in tears because the neighborhood rowdies
had taken the money his mother gave him to buy milk. He complained
to his older brother, Sam. The older brother felt bad for the little guy
and gave him money to replace the amount that was stolen.

The younger brother got angry. His brother asked him, "Why are
you angry?"

"I want you to go and beat them up, and get my milk money back!"

"I've just given you exactly what they took from you. Why do you
have the right to be angry?"

"They deserve to get beat up. They were wrong to take my money.
They need to get punished, and I want you to go beat them up!"

"This is the way I decided to fix the wrong done to you. If I go beat
those kids up, I'm just as bad as them. The money wasn't yours in the
first place, Mom gave it to you. Why are you so angry? Your anger is
just as bad as them stealing."

The younger brother went away sad and angry because his older
brother wouldn't fix the situation the way his emotions wanted them
fixed. He didn't care about right and wrong; he wanted the kids who
took his money punished.

We are that way many times when we pray to God to take vengeance on people because they hurt us, lied to us, frightened us, gossiped about us, or took something from us.

No one ever gets away with wrong. God eventually judges even the intentions and thoughts in our hearts and minds. We should tell God our problems, and when He comes up with solutions, we should accept His wisdom and thank Him for taking care of us in all things— even those painful situations when wrong was done to us or those we love.

> Forgive me, Lord, when I wish to take Your
> place, usurp Your authority in my life, and wreak
> vengeance on others. Give me a forgiving heart,
> dear Lord. Amen.

Fat Cat

And no marvel; for Satan himself is transformed
into an angel of light.
—2 Corinthians 11:14 (KJV)

Be sober, be vigilant; because your adversary the
devil, as a roaring lion, walketh about, seeking
whom he may devour:
—1 Peter 5:8 (KJV)

I was visiting my sister's cottage and noticed her beautiful, huge, snow-white tomcat. He was absolutely harmless as he was declawed, neutered, and so old he was deaf. He was pretty stupid, also. He would sit for hours under her bird feeders and crouch down to watch the birds eat. Every day he lay still for hours, watch those birds eat the free food my sister put out for them daily.

I couldn't help comparing him to that old "fat cat" Satan. He can come disguised as an angel of light, but if you're close to the Lord, you will recognize him.

Jesus Christ declawed Satan at the cross on Calvary. He has no power over us in the areas of sin and death ever again if we believe in Jesus Christ.

Jesus Christ neutered Satan. He can never produce others like himself. He can only keep what he obtained in the garden of Eden, and even they who choose to go up to Jesus's side will be saved forever. So all Satan can do is try to hang on to what he already has.

Satan's tricks are as old as the universe. He is deaf and cannot hear our thoughts and hearts. We are safe feeding on the Word of God daily as long as we stay up in the area of Jesus, away from Satan's reach. But be warned: if you go down to his level and think you can be safe, you are wrong. Satan still has vicious teeth that can tear you to shreds if you venture into his territory.

Stay high and close to Jesus. Feed on the free Word of God every day. Satan roams around, looking for a helpless Christian to devour. Stay out of his reach.

Jesus, thank You so much that You won my victory
and keep me high and lifted away from this world
and Satan. Amen.

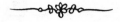

Namesake

He leads me in the paths of righteousness for His
name's sake.

—Psalm 23:3 (NKJV)

I have a namesake. My best friend had a baby daughter, and because of my friend's great love for me, she named her precious daughter after me.

God Almighty has an only begotten Son. His name is Jesus Christ. If you belong to God Almighty by accepting Jesus Christ as your Savior, you have a new name! God has named you after His Son, you are a Christian.

It is for His name's sake that God Almighty will keep you in paths of righteousness. If you bear the name Christian, you are special and set apart. You are a child of God. God will not allow you to sully His name or the name of His Son, Jesus Christ.

Many times my children moaned to me, "Mom, all the other kids get to do this, that, or the other!"

I would say, "Those are not my kids. I will not let you do that. You are part of this family, and you will not make our name look bad with your actions!"

Well, listen to the Father. He will not allow His holy name to be defiled by your actions. He will not let the holy name of Jesus Christ be stained by your poor example. You are a namesake. If you bear the family name of Christian, be one. If you are not going to bear the name with honor, give up the name.

> What a precious namesake I bear. Thank You, God,
> that You lead me in the right path in this world for
> Your name's sake. Amen.

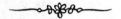

Snow and Rainbows

Come now, and let us reason together, saith the
Lord: though your sins be as scarlet, they shall be as
white as snow;
—Isaiah 1:18 (KJV)

And He that sat was to look upon like a jasper and a
sardine stone: and there was a rainbow round about
the throne, in sight like unto an emerald.
—Revelation 4:3 (KJV)

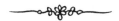

Our small group was out riding our bicycles one day in early spring.
We were in winter shape and just starting to try to get these bodies we
say belong to the Lord into better condition. We know these bodies
are God's and that we are in charge of them. After all, they have to
last us a lifetime.

We were getting very tired about two-thirds of the way into a
fifteen-mile ride. Lungs were straining, leg muscles were screaming,
and our hearts felt like they were bursting. Our backsides weren't
feeling too good, either.

Suddenly, the clouds became an ominous black. It started to snow
and sleet. *Great,* I thought, *just what we need.*

One rider stopped abruptly in the middle of the bike path and
shouted for us to look up. We all stopped and looked up. There was
a rainbow in the break in the clouds. What awesome beauty. We all
began to "ooh," "ahh," and smile. We were immediately revived and

encouraged by the beauty of the Lord's earth. With renewed energy we finish the remainder of the ride in great spirits.

After I came home and began to write in my journal, I thought about our ride. I pondered about my sins being washed whiter than snow by my Lord Jesus's perfect blood. I thought of the rainbow surrounding God's throne in heaven.

This day turned out to be the most beautiful day. I felt exhilarated. Why? Because my Jesus had taken the time to encourage me with the beauty of His nature and who He is—all because a friend encouraged me to look up.

Lord Jesus, may I be faithful to encourage others
to look up to You for beauty, hope, and joy in this
world. Amen.

Suffering and Rejoicing

Nay, much more those members of the body, which
seem to be more feeble, are necessary: And those
members of the body, which we think to be less
honourable, upon these we bestow more abundant
honour; and our uncomely parts have more
abundant comeliness. For our comely parts have no
need: but God hath tempered the body together,
having given more abundant honour to that part
which lacked: That there should be no schism in the
body; but that the members should have the same
care one for another. And whether one member
suffer, all the members suffer with it; or one member
be honoured, all the members rejoice with it. Now ye
are the body of Christ, and members in particular.
—1 Corinthians 12:22–27 (KJV)

I rushed to a philosophy class at college. I was excited. I was doing a
comparison of Plato's philosophy to modern-day Christianity and was
the key speaker for the day. My impatient nature caused me to bypass
the elevator and challenge the stairs. Painful choice.

I had a thirty-five-pound book bag on my shoulder and wore
high-heeled shoes to complement my business suit. I wanted to look
distinguished. Well, to make a painful story shorter, the heel of my
shoe caught in the metal grid of the stairs, and in quite an undignified
way, down I went. I broke my left ankle in two places. Ouch!

The injury required a cast from the hip to the toes. During my time of healing, I learned a valuable lesson about the body. My useless left leg had to be carried around by the rest of my body. My right leg became muscular and strong. My hands became calloused from the crutches. My armpits were sore, but my arms began to form muscles in places I didn't even know existed. My sense of balance changed for six weeks so I didn't go headlong down flights of stairs. Taking a bath was an entirely irritating yet humorous endeavor.

What a lesson! Let me parallel this to the body of Christ. My "less honorable broken ankle" was not ignored. If it had been, there would have been pain throughout my body. As a matter of fact, that ankle was pampered for six weeks of healing and then again for about three months for strengthening and to become fully useful again. We should do this for those weak members of the body of Christ; don't ignore, but pamper them back to full strength.

If you are that good right leg doing all the work, think of the added strength you obtain by carrying around the weaker part. If you are the hands or arms, think of the added muscle you are gaining in your spiritual life. If you are those overworked armpits, just think of the balance you have afforded the body so it would not be cast headlong into danger. Washing weaker members in the water of the Word can be irritating but very humorous at times.

Note what the verses say about the body: "And whether one member suffer, all the members suffer with it; or one member be honoured, all the members rejoice with it." Every part of my body needed all other parts of my body. My whole body suffered. Each part of my body rejoiced in good health after we all strengthened and healed together.

Note the passage does not say when one member suffers you all ought to suffer or when one member rejoices you all ought to rejoice. It says, "all should suffer, all should rejoice."

Thanks, Lord, for a painful but accurate picture of
the body of Christ. Amen.

Abba Father

And he said, Abba, Father, all things are possible
unto thee; take away this cup from me: nevertheless
not what I will, but what thou wilt.
—Mark 14:36 (KJV)

For ye have not received the spirit of bondage again
to fear; but ye have received the Spirit of adoption,
whereby we cry, Abba, Father.
—Romans 8:15 (KJV)

And because ye are sons, God hath sent forth the
Spirit of his Son into your hearts, crying, Abba,
Father.
—Galatians 4:6 (KJV)

I stood on the mountain overlooking the Mount of Olives, looking
toward the eastern gate of Jerusalem. I was amazed to be in the land
where my Lord had walked, ministered, and died. All of a sudden I
heard a small voice below me plaintively cry, "Abba! Abba! Abba!" As
I looked down into the park below me, I saw two small boys playing.

It was evident their daddy was oblivious to the harassment his
older son was meting out to his younger son as Daddy sat with his
headset on, enjoying his music. I watched in amusement until the
younger son finally caught his daddy's eye and cried louder, "Abba!
Abba! Abba!"

The dad took hold of his younger son, drew him onto his lap, and said some severe words of reprimand to his older son. The older son, with downcast eyes, sat down and ceased harassing his baby brother. The younger son sat on Daddy's lap and enjoyed his comfort from Abba.

I put myself in the place of that small child. How many times has someone or something harassed me and I ran to my heavenly Father and pled for Him to make my tormentor leave me alone? How many times have I been pulled into the lap of my heavenly Father and been comforted and loved?

What a beautiful example in Scripture for Jesus to cry out to the Father and call Him Daddy! How very blessed we are to have the privilege because of the death of Jesus Christ, God's Son, to be able to call a holy God, Daddy.

Climb up on His lap today and talk to Him. God loves it when you call Him Abba, Father, Daddy, God.

Thank You, Jesus, for making it possible for me
to be in the family of God and call a holy God my
Abba. Amen.

Living Water

Now on the last day, the great day of the feast,
Jesus stood and cried out, saying, If anyone thirsts,
let him come to Me and drink. He who believes
into Me, as the Scripture said, out of his innermost
being shall flow rivers of living water
—John 7:37 (NIV)

When I was in Israel, I stood by the Dead Sea, wondering why it was dead and stagnant. Fresh water flows into it from the north, but there is no outlet at its tip.

It is like that with many Christians. They go to God daily for a fresh supply of living water, but they never let it flow out to others. They become dead and stagnant in their Christian walk and witness.

Others may tell you, "You have to be a channel of living water. You should be one with the Holy Spirit so the living water—the Holy Spirit—can flow into you."

However, a channel has two ends. The channel of the Holy Spirit, this channel of life, also has two ends. One end is toward the Holy Spirit, toward life, and toward the Lord. The other end is toward humankind. Living water will never flow if the end toward humankind is closed.

No one can be so wrong as to assume that just opening to the Lord is enough. Living water does not flow through those who are opened just to the Lord. One end must be open to the Lord, and the other end must be open to humankind. Living water will flow out only when both ends are open. Many people are powerless before God because the end toward the Lord is not open. But many more people are powerless because the end for witnessing and leading others to Christ is closed.

> For whosoever shall give you a cup of water to
> drink in my name, because ye belong to Christ,
> verily I say unto you, he shall not lose his reward.
> (Mark 9:41 KJV)

Lord Jesus, please let us not hoard the living water
of Your Holy Spirit for our own selfish pleasures.
Help us open our hearts and let the living water
of the Spirit of God flow out to others and quench
their thirsty souls. Help us to have a constant flow
of living water into our spirits for our own spiritual
thirst, and let us release it for others to drink freely
of the Spirit of God. Amen.

White as Snow

Come now, and let us reason together, saith the
Lord: though your sins be as scarlet, they shall be
as white as snow; though they be red like crimson,
they shall be as wool.

—Isaiah 1:18 (KJV)

As I looked out my window today, I almost got discouraged. It's
snowing again! I thought of the words the prophet Isaiah wrote so
many years ago. What lesson could it teach me today? What spiritual
insight was God trying to place into my heart?

As I peered out my picture window, I noticed the light reflecting
on the snow, making it dazzlingly pure white. I stood and meditated.
The snow totally covered all the dirt of my part of the earth. Everything
looked pure and clean. The light reflected off the snow in a brilliant
beauty back up into the sky!

Wow! This was a picture of Jesus Christ, my Savior
and Redeemer! I remembered the verses in the
book of Matthew, Mark, and Luke, where the Lord
Jesus was transfigured before the eyes of Peter,
James, and John. They saw Him reflecting the
glory of God. "And his raiment became shining,
exceeding white as snow; so as no fuller on earth
can white them."

—Mark 9:3 (KJV)

Isaiah prophesied of the cleansing power of Jesus
Christ, and the apostles saw this cleansing person.
Then I remembered that in the book of Revelation,

the apostle John saw this cleansing, risen Savior
standing in the middle of the churches: "His head
and his hairs were white like wool, as white as
snow; and his eyes were as a flame of fire;"
—Revelation 1:14 (KJV)

What a lesson snow can teach us. Are we allowing the Lord to reason with our hearts to deal with our sins so He can wash us and make us white as snow? Are we allowing the Lord Jesus Christ to live through us so we send the reflected white as snow glory of God out to the world and back up to God the Father? Are we standing up for the white as snow Head of the church, the Lord Jesus Christ, proclaiming Him and Him alone? The Lord can use all His creation to proclaim His Word, even something as white as snow.

Thank You, Jesus, for cleansing me and taking away
the stain of sin and making me as white as the snow
through You. Amen.

Light or Soot?

Ye are the light of the world. A city that is set on a
hill cannot be hid. Neither do men light a candle,
and put it under a bushel, but on a candlestick; and
it giveth light unto all that are in the house.
—Matthew 5:14–15 (KJV)

I love candles and have them all over my house. I like the warm
atmosphere when I have them all lit. I love the fragrance they give
off. Today I was rushing to make an appointment. I was negative and
in a foul mood. I went around snuffing out all the candles for safety's
sake. With each puff, the light of the candle went out, and a cloud of
soot spiraled upward.

I stopped dead in my tracks. The verses above went through my
head and fell like a rock into my heart. I realized I was not giving off
light. I was oozing soot.

Jesus said He was the light of the world, and I am supposed to
reflect Him. My negativity and foul mood were spiraling sin soot
directly up to my Lord.

I was hiding the light of my Savior under the bushel of my human
feelings. If someone were to encounter me, all he or she would see was
the soot of a light I had extinguished by negative thinking. That soot
of negativity and a foul mood would contaminate anyone I came in
contact with.

I spoke out loud, "Lord, forgive me!" Immediately I felt the warm
glow of the light of the Lord illumine my heart. I smiled. I went out to
my appointment with the Lord's light in my heart.

Thank You, Lord, for immediate rekindling! Amen.

Work-Worn Hands Are Blessed Hands

(Published in *Mature Years* magazine, 2004–2005)

Blessed is every one that feareth the Lord; that
walketh in his ways. For thou shalt eat the labour
of thine hands: happy shalt thou be, and it shall be
well with thee. Thy wife shall be as a fruitful vine
by the sides of thine house: thy children like olive
plants round about thy table. Behold, that thus shall
the man be blessed that feareth the Lord.

—Psalm 128:1–4 (KJV)

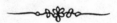

We were in Toronto, Canada, celebrating our wedding anniversary.
We were prepared for a very fancy anniversary dinner. I did a familiar
thing. I placed my hands up in the middle of the table. This was a
prompt for my husband to reach over and cover my hands, which are
half the size of his, with his hands. It's our love language when in a
public place.

The table was covered with a white, linen tablecloth. He reached
up and placed his hands over mine. Almost immediately, he removed
his hands and placed them on his lap, out of sight. I asked him, "What's
wrong?"

He said, "I saw my hands on that white tablecloth and realized
how beat up and dirty they looked. I felt ashamed of them."

I felt a pain in my heart that forced me to speak very quietly to this man I love. I told him, "Sam, I love you more than words can ever say. I have never been ashamed of anything about you my entire life. I placed my life in those hands when I was a young bride. It is those hands that have earned a living for us all these years. It is those hands that have held all our babies, put together toys, fixed cars, built a home, and a thousand other things. It is those hands that have held and caressed me when I was sick or hurt or crying. Don't ever be ashamed of those hands. They are a blessing in my life."

Tenderness came over his face. I saw the awkwardness of the action, but up from under the table came his hands. He covered my small hands with his huge, work-worn hands. He looked me straight in the face and simply said, "I love you."

My heart pain went away. I said, "I love you, too."

Praise You, Lord Jesus, that You gave me a perfect
soul mate in this life under the sun. Thank You for
the hardworking and precious husband You have
given me. Amen.

In His Image

Be ye therefore imitators of God, as beloved
children.
—Ephesians 5:1 (KJV)

My husband and our two teen sons stood in front of our six-foot wide bathroom mirror. We installed that mirror because we had three daughters, two sons, and one bathroom. Mirror space for makeup for the girls and shaving for the guys was a necessity, so share it was.

I stood outside the open door and chuckled. The guys all stood exactly the same as they shaved. Right foot sitting on top of the left foot, head tilted, mouth pulled to the right or the left, depending on which side of the face was being shaved.

I have watched my husband shave for many years, and I knew our sons had picked up their dad's habits in more areas than shaving. Why? They looked up to their dad. They imitated him in every way possible, even in ways they were not aware of. Why? Because he loved them and spent time with them, and they loved him and spent time with him. They took on his very actions and nature as sons.

It's that way with God the Father. The more you hang out with, love, and look up to Him, the more you will become like Him. Want to know what He looks like, acts like, and what His attributes are? Go look in the Word. He sent His Son, Jesus. Jesus was the image of the Father. We have our role model.

God hath in these last days spoken unto us by his
Son, whom He hath appointed heir of all things,
by whom also he made the worlds; Who being the
brightness of His glory, and the express image of
His person, and upholding all things by the word of
His power. (Hebrews 1:2–3 KJV)

Thank You, Father, for Your Word, Jesus, and Your
written Word to show us how to be imitators of
You. Amen.

Grandma's Quilt

Then He spoke a parable to them: "No one puts a
piece from a new garment on an old one; otherwise
the new makes a tear, and also the piece that was
taken out of the new does not match the old."
—Luke 5:36–39 (NKJV)

My daughter Cristi Ana has a quilt her grandmother made her many years ago. She used to walk around the house with that quilt wrapped around her. She is married now.

One day she came over with this beat-up, ratty, torn, soiled quilt and gave it to me. "Mom, can you fix this?" I told her it looked like a hopeless case. There was quite a bit of damage and plain old wear and tear. "But Mom, Grandma made me that quilt, and I really love it. Please see what you can do."

I laid that quilt on the living room floor and walked around it for a day, trying to figure out what to do. To me it looked hopeless. Her dad was sitting on the sofa, looking at the quilt, and said quite plainly, "Well, if you want it to be as nearly like the original, you'll have to take out all the ripped and damaged pieces, and start from the beginning."

Now he doesn't quilt, so he didn't know how much work was involved. What he was telling me, in essence, was to cut out all the destroyed pieces, take the patchwork apart from the middle batting, take off the backing, repair all the damaged pieces in the middle of the patchwork with the original pieces, gently put the top patching over the middle batting, wrap the backing around the two, hand tack the three pieces together, and then hem all three into one again. In other words, I must remake the entire quilt with all the original pieces.

I got started. As I was repairing, I pondered how much I loved my daughter. I joked with my son that she was a spoiled brat, though I loved every minute of what I was doing. I could anticipate her face when she looked at Grandma's quilt, totally restored. After all the work was done, I washed the quilt. When I pulled the quilt out of the dryer I got such a feeling of satisfaction.

This morning I was reading the Word and got a great picture in my heart. I could see Jesus Christ laying us out and pondering our damaged lives. He never thinks a person is hopeless. The Father tells Jesus, "Well, you must take out all the damaged pieces and start from the beginning."

Jesus lovingly begins. He takes out a damaged piece here and gently places a piece there. He goes into the middle of our beings and repairs our damaged emotions. It takes Him a lifetime, but as we are being restored He carefully puts us back together, and all three parts of us—body, soul, and spirit—become one because of His work.

Our original bodies, souls, and spirits are restored. He has washed us as white as snow What a feeling of satisfaction our Lord must feel when He has restored us with His loving lifetime touch.

Now may the God of peace Himself sanctify you completely; and may your whole spirit, soul, and body be preserved blameless at the coming of our Lord Jesus Christ. (1 Thessalonians 5:23 NKJV)

Thank You so much, Lord Jesus, that You repaired our damages. Thank You for restoring us to be like You. Amen.

He Is a Rock; I Am a Rock

He only is my rock and my salvation: he is my
defense; I shall not be moved. In God is my
salvation and my glory: the rock of my strength,
and my refuge, is in God.
—Psalm 62:6–7 (KJV)

I picked up a small rock on the rugged coastal shoreline of Maine. It's worn smooth from the oils of my hands as I rub it while I pray or meditate or even when I am worrying and fretting about things I can't change.

My rock is not particularly beautiful. There is nothing about it that caused me to choose it because it was so special. If I were to throw it back on the earth, nothing would set it apart from all the other rocks. But my attention was drawn to that particular rock, and I have carried it with me ever since as a reminder.

What does this rock remind me of? I am reminded that I am like that small rock. I am not particularly beautiful. There is nothing about me that would cause anyone to choose me. There is nothing that sets me apart from all others.

Still, my Lord reached down to earth and chose me out of all the others. He carries me with Him at all times. All the jagged edges of humanity are being worn smooth by the touch of my Master's hand and the oil of His Holy Spirit. He prays for me, meditates over me, frets over me, and worries over me.

God has to constantly remind me He is my salvation. He is my defense. He is my glory. He is the rock of my strength. He is my refuge. I am just a tiny, human rock in the hands of a mighty God. I am content to lay in the palm of His hand and be conformed by my mighty rock into His very image.

> Thank You, Rock, for my salvation, for calling me to Your mighty love and shelter, and choosing me and filling me with Your Holy Spirit. Amen.

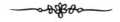

Living Water or Polluted Water

For my people have committed two evils; they
have forsaken me the fountain of living waters, and
hewed them out cisterns, broken cisterns, that can
hold no water.

—Jeremiah 2:13 (KJV)

At 4:11 p.m. on August 14, 2003, the power went off. It was the result of a widespread power outage in the Northeast and Midwestern United States and the province of Ontario, Canada. It made me realize all the toys and gadgets we have that are our idols.

After a very uncomfortable, no air-conditioned, no electronic gadgets to amuse myself, and dark evening, I went to bed.

I woke up at about 2 a.m. and went to the bathroom. As is my habit, I drank a huge glass of cold tap water, chugging it down without taking a breath. It tasted horrible. The next morning I heard on the news that we were supposed to boil our water. The water filtration plant is powered by electricity, and since there was no electricity, our water was polluted and unsafe for drinking. Needless to say, I had an upset stomach, headache, and various other discomforts all day long.

So where is this story going? Well, are our luxuries sometimes our idols? Do we settle for the polluted water from the broken cisterns of our luxurious little gods? Do we drink from this world's waters of pleasure and cause ourselves to become sin sick?

Have we become too comfortable in this world and forsaken the Lord while pretending to serve Him? Have we hewed out cisterns—broken cisterns of luxury—that have become our gods yet do not water out thirsty spirits?

In Jeremiah's day, the children of Israel made their own gods and worshipped them instead of the living God who delivered them from bondage and supplied them with manna from heaven and water from the Rock. The Lord called their idols "cisterns, broken cisterns."

I was physically sick from drinking polluted water. Think of all the people who are spiritually sick and will die eternally if they do not get a drink of that living water. They drink the polluted water from the broken cisterns of the world every day and remain sin sick. It is our responsibility to be ambassadors for Jesus Christ, the living water.

Have you given anyone a cup of living water lately? Have you had a cup of that refreshing living water yourself? Go get a cup, and share it with someone.

Almighty God, I praise You and glorify You for
sending the living water and manna from heaven in
the person of my Lord and Savior, Jesus Christ.

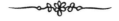

Cancer: A Gift?

And lest I should be exalted above measure through
the abundance of the revelations, there was given
to me a thorn in the flesh, the messenger of Satan to
buffet me, lest I should be exalted above measure.
For this thing I besought the Lord thrice, that it
might depart from me. And he said unto me, My
grace is sufficient for thee: for my strength is made
perfect in weakness. Most gladly therefore will I
rather glory in my infirmities, that the power of
Christ may rest upon me.
—2 Corinthians 12:7–9 (KJV)

A beautiful Christian college professor and mentor of mine went through cancer, chemo, and extreme sickness. When she speaks of it, she calls her cancer, "her gift from God."

My soul rebelled at this. I thought, *God doesn't do this to people; Satan does.* I had a lot to learn about grace, strength, and power.

Her flesh was the only part that was harmed. Her spirit, which belongs to God, was made strong by her pulling on the strength of the Lord to make it through this cancer. She felt the grace of God carry her through the cancer. Her teaching now reflects a much greater power than human power. It exhibits God's Holy Spirit power to a much greater degree than before.

Satan cannot do anything to a child of God with our God's permission. If God allows sickness to enter your flesh, He is giving you an opportunity for His power to be brought forth from your spirit. He is encouraging you to pull on His strength and not your own. Through His grace, you will live out your days in victory over Satan in your spirit.

The flesh belongs to Satan, and it will rot in the grave. But things done in your spirit will follow you into eternity. Just like the apostle Paul, she can now say, "Therefore most gladly I will rather boast in my infirmities, that the power of Christ may rest upon me." (II Corinthians 12:9 NKJV) Or, "My cancer was a gift from God."

I now realize she was given an immeasurable gift of love from God in allowing something He knew would draw her even closer into His heart. The strength, power, and grace with which she went through her ordeal with cancer opened the hearts of doctors, nurses, technicians, and other cancer patients.

I love you, Doc Teri!

Thank You for allowing discomfort, pain, and suffering into my human life for the purpose of drawing me closer to You, and to be an example and witness for those who watch as I stay strong in my Lord. Amen.

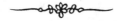

Whale-Sized Feeding

Am I a sea, or a whale, that thou settest a watch
over me?
—Job 7:12 (KJV)

How sweet are thy words unto my taste! yea,
sweeter than honey to my mouth!
—Psalm 119:103 (KJV)

Humpbacked whales are mammals that give birth to their young and suckle them with their own milk. Calves are born tail-first or they die. When it emerges from the mother, a midwife whale pushes the calf up to the top of the water so it can take its first breath.

The calf weighs five thousand pounds and is ten to fifteen feet long. The mother humpback is forty to fifty feet long and weighs one ton per foot of length. She eats two thousand to three thousand pounds of food per day. Do you know what this huge creature eats? She eats small krill, small shrimp, and small crustaceans.

She takes in tons of water at a gulp and closes her mouth. Her baleen plates excrete all the water and leave the small creatures she has gulped on her tongue. She does this many times a day. She takes in huge amounts to get that small morsel of food. Is God awesome or what?

We are like that humpback whale. God sets a watch over us. We feed on His Word. The Holy Spirit is our baleen plates. We take in tons of food through our eyes, ears, and emotions per day. The Holy Spirit excretes the unnecessary, unspiritual food, leaving a sweet morsel of spiritual food on our tongues to feed our spirits time and time again throughout the day. Is God awesome or what?

> Praise You, God, for the awesome things You have created with the power of Your Word alone. Thank You for watching over me in all areas of my human existence. Amen.

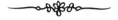

Soar into Death

Yea, though I walk through the valley of the shadow
of death, I will fear no evil; For You are with me;
—Psalm 23:4 (NKJV)

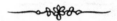

A butterfly lays its eggs on a moist green leaves so when the larva appears, it will have life and nourishment. The larva attaches itself to the leaf and becomes a cocoon, wrapping protection around its body. It will live on that leaf until it matures.

A miraculous thing then happens. The cocoon bursts open, and a wet, weak creature struggles out of the cocoon. The more it struggles, the stronger it gets. It totters out on the stem or branch of the tree and allows its wings to dry and become strong.

It becomes beautiful. Its vivid colors appear. It is graceful and ready to become airborne. The wings of the wind are there, and it soars up into the heavens. It was not brought to life to live in a cocoon on a leaf for the rest of its life.

We are that way. We live in the cocoon of our bodies. This is where we have physical life and are nourished in our souls. But there comes a day when we burst out of our cocoons and realize we weren't destined to stay on this earth. We struggle to free ourselves of this human cocoon called a body, and the death process begins.

The world sees a weak, wet creature that looks as if it is dying. The Lord sees a beautiful loved one, sitting on earth and waiting to be beckoned to Him. We struggle against death. We get strong enough to trust His call.

We take off with the wings of the Spirit. We soar into the heavens and take a quick look back at our cocoons. We wonder why we held on to its protection so long. We look up. There is our God. Nothing can compare to the beauty in Him and paradise!

We realize He was with us all through the valley of the shadow of death—from the day we took our first breaths until the day we exhaled our last. We must walk that lonesome valley, but we do not have to walk it by ourselves. This is called the earth pilgrimage, and all must take it.

> Lord God Almighty, praise You that You are with
> me in the weakness of my body. You sustain me
> with nourishment from Your Word. Praise You that
> You are making me beautiful for Your own glory.
> Amen.

Appointed or Disappointed

And the king's servants said unto the king, Behold,
thy servants are ready to do whatsoever my lord the
king shall appoint.
—2 Samuel 15:15 (KJV)

I had a deep disappointment. I applied for a job I thought was perfect for me. It was right down my line of experience and training. It was in a Christian environment. I interviewed with the people and really liked them. The hours were perfect. I had been laid off for over a year, and we could really use the money. I did not get the job. I still don't know exactly why.

Today I read this verse. It is talking about the time King David's son Absalom usurped the throne. King David's loyal followers said, "Behold, thy servants are ready to do whatsoever my lord the king shall appoint."

King David's entire group fled into the wilderness until God took care of the situation. Notice God took care of the situation, not King David and his followers. King David specifically gave the situation over to his God.

God is my King. If I truly believe He cares for me and watches over me, I must believe He appointed this in my life. I must believe He has the perfect job, not just a really good job, somewhere else. I must trust He knows me better than I know myself, and He has my best interests at heart. I must let God take care of the situation.

Have you had an appointment you wanted and did not get? Have you experienced a disappointment because God said no to something? Take heart. God knows you better than you know yourself. He will give you exactly what is best for your life at this point in time. Be gracious with the Lord's will for your life. The Father knows best.

Lord, I give the appointments, disappointments
over to Your all-knowing care and love of Your
child. Amen.

Unthankful

But love ye your enemies, and do good, and lend,
hoping for nothing again; and your reward shall be
great, and ye shall be the children of the Highest:
for He is kind unto the unthankful and to the evil.
—Luke 6:35 (KJV)

I was sad and blue. It was Thanksgiving, and I had to work. I had totally forgotten God gave me this job. I was disappointed by not getting a job I thought was perfect. God graciously gave me one I liked even better, working in the behavioral health-care unit of a hospital two miles from my home.

The rookies at a hospital always have to work holidays! It just didn't seem quite fair. I wanted to spend Thanksgiving with my family. It is my favorite holiday.

I looked at a picture of my five children on the wall. It was a collage of them all at about age three. They are now adults and have lives of their own. The first picture said, "When they are young, we look ahead." The last caption said, "When they are older, our hearts look back." I cried in self-pity. Even if I didn't have to work, everyone had other plans.

Suddenly, I remembered. I had asked the Lord for this job. He honored me by not only giving me the schooling to accomplish it, He got me a job two miles away from home in the hospital I had wanted to work in for over twenty years.

I thought of the patients I would be with today. *They are not home with their families, either.* I felt the sting of my selfishness. I realized God is kind to me even when I am unthankful toward Him. My family is still my family even when they have other commitments. God has just broadened my family.

I asked God to forgive my selfishness. It is now time to nourish my servanthood and give my love in the area God provided. I asked Him to let me go to work with a positive and thankful attitude.

I prayed He lets me be an encouragement to someone today. As I fulfill my work commitment today, let me expect nothing in return. Thanksgiving has taken on a different face, but it is still my favorite holiday.

Please forgive my selfish, unthankful heart, and put
a heart of love and caring there for this new family
you have placed in my life. Amen.

Man in the Mirror

For if anyone is a hearer of the word and not a
doer, he is like a man observing his natural face in
a mirror; for he observes himself, goes away, and
immediately forgets what kind of man he was.

—James 1:23–25 (NKJV)

I worked in the psychiatric ward of a hospital. One of the functions I did was something called Q 15s. Q 15 means you must locate the patient every fifteen minutes and verify where the patient is and what the patient is doing. The information is documented on the patient's medical chart. This is for safety reasons for those on suicide, homicide, falls, and medical precautions.

One night I was making my rounds and came to a room that housed two patients. Only one of them was on Q 15s. I heard someone talking very softly. He was saying, "You don't want to kill me. Come on now. You know you don't want to kill me, man. Just stop now. You don't have to do this. You know you don't hate me. Don't do it, man. I'm not a bad sort of guy."

My heart began to beat very fast. I looked for the red security alert button located in many locations on our unit. There was one just inside the door of the patient's room.

I peeked around the door only to see that one of the patients was fast asleep in his bed. The other patient's bed was empty. The talk was coming from the patient bathroom.

I stole a glance around the corner and saw the patient talking to his image in the stainless steel mirror. I called his name gently, with one hand poised near the red button. He turned, looked at me, and asked what I wanted. I suggested he come out to the day area and watch TV. He obediently followed. The patient said nothing of the incident; indeed, he seemed to have forgotten it completely. I reported it and duly wrote it on the patient's chart.

What a lesson from the Holy Spirit of God hit my heart. Our flesh and spirits have this fight every single moment of every single day. We go to the mirror of God's Word and see what we really are. If we are a hearer and not a doer, we immediately go on our way and forget the real us we saw in the pages of God's Word.

We tell ourselves we don't want to kill our sinful flesh and let our spirits rule. We say we don't have to do things we don't want to do. We convince ourselves we aren't such bad people after all. We love our flesh more than we love the spirit God breathed into us to overcome the world.

Our red button is prayer. Jesus said so in Mark 14:37–39 (NKJV): "Watch and pray, lest you enter into temptation. The spirit truly is willing, but the flesh is weak."

Father God, help me to look faithfully into the
mirror of Your Word, and obey what it says for the
growth of my spirit and to curb the sinful desires of
my flesh. Amen.

Wash Me

Wash me, and I shall be whiter than snow.
—Psalm 51:7 (NIV)

Jesus answered him, "If I do not wash you, you have
no part with Me."
—John 13:8 (NIV)

Last night was a very rough night in the behavioral health-care unit where I work. We were nonstop busy with admits and discharges. All the patients seemed to be extra needy emotionally and physically. My body ached from all the lifting, bathing, changing, feeding, gluco scanning, bed making, and so on. Then we got an admit who was very pitiful.

He was old, unkempt, disoriented, and the filthiest human being I had ever encountered. Please forgive my blunt honesty in the next few sentences, but this is what I do and the only way I can explain it.

After his assessment by the medical staff, he was handed over to the state-tested nursing assistant (STNA), that would be me, for orienting to the unit. Part of orientation is to get the patient cleaned up and established in a room.

I donned the gloves and the plastic gown. I took the patient into the huge walk-in shower. I literally peeled off his clothing and sat him on a bath chair. I began to scrub. It took five washcloths lathered with antibacterial soap to clean the feces from his buttocks and the filth from his body. I gently pushed back the foreskin, and he was bleeding and red from infection. I was as gentle as I could be. I shampooed the scaly substance from his gray hair. I lathered the scruffy beard and gave him a shave.

After cleaning and rinsing for about half an hour, I began to pat him dry. All this time, he was totally compliant. Except for having to hold him up because of his unstableness, he tried to be helpful.

I got him into bed and went one-tenth of a mile to the other end of the hospital to get an EKG machine. I rushed back to the patient's room, attach the lead wires, and get a reading for the doctor who requested it. I see the results first. There is a problem with his heart. I pray in my heart, *Okay, Lord, what is the lesson from this experience? I know You have one.*

I felt a divine chuckle form deep in my heart. The Lord asked me, *What do you think you looked like when I found you, before I held up your unstable physical being and washed you of the filth of the world? What do you think I found when I checked your heart? I washed you with My very own blood and placed a new heart in you.*

Somehow my evening wasn't so bad after all.

Thank You, Lord Jesus, for cleaning me up and
placing a spiritual heart in me. Thank You for those
You bring under my care. Help me love them with a
love only You can give. Amen.

Treasures

Do not store up for yourselves treasures on earth,
where moth and rust destroy, and where thieves
break in and steal. But store up for yourselves
treasures in heaven, where moth and rust do not
destroy, and where thieves do not break in and
steal. For where your treasure is, there your heart
will be also.

—Matthew 6:19–21 (NIV)

But we have this treasure in jars of clay to show
that this all-surpassing power is from God and not
from us.

—2 Corinthians 4:7 (NIV)

Strong's Greek: thesauros, a deposit

It was New Year's Eve, and I was working in the behavioral health-care unit. I asked myself, *What is the greatest treasure I have from this year?* I do this every year. I think back over the year. I reflect on my life. I read my daily journal, my walk with God. I pray. I worship. I look forward with anticipation to the New Year with God. What will He do?

I go back to a patient in the psychiatric ward where I worked this year. He raised a ruckus! He ripped phones out of the wall. He cursed. He was a retired firefighter and must have been about six feet six inches tall.

He tied his oxygen tubes into knots just for the fun of it. He broke beds. He ripped drawer fronts off. He answered patient's shared phone with, "Joe's Bar, Joe speaking!" and then roar with laughter because the person assumed he or she had the wrong number. He then sang at the top of his lungs, "In heaven there is no beer; that's why we drink it here!"

Not many workers wanted him as a patient. I purposefully chose him when I had the choice. God gave him to me. I tried many times to find the courage to talk to him about God. I failed miserably. I loved him, but I was afraid in some way to tell him how much God loved him, so I just loved him myself.

He ended up in intensive care. I visited him, but he was so drugged he could not respond. I prayed for him and asked God for forgiveness for failing to witness to him. He disappeared after about three weeks, and I assumed he had died. I had failed.

I received a commission from the hospital, volunteer pastoral care. During my rounds I saw a name that was not on my list to visit— the ruckus-raising firefighter. He was alive! I went there first.

There was a huge red stop sign, which meant you can't go in without the nurse saying it is okay. I asked her, "What do I need to do to visit?"

She looked at my badge and said, "Suit up! Gown, gloves, mask." I did.

When I saw him, my heart sank about five thousand miles. He had a tracheotomy, a colostomy, a folly, and many tubes and wires. He was so skinny. He looked at me with a blank stare. I asked, "Hey, do you remember me?" He couldn't talk because of the tracheotomy, but he shook his head. How could he recognize me? I had a mask covering my face.

I didn't feel stupid or afraid this time. I just belted out, "In heaven there is no beer; that's why we drink it here." I didn't even care what the nurse thought. She was cleaning his trach tube. Big tears welled up in his eyes. He remembered me as his caregiver in the behavioral health-care unit!

The nurse told me he had cancer and was undergoing radiation treatments. I told her how I knew him. She said, "Good. You can help me with him." We cleaned, we changed, we rolled. We even shifted his six-foot six-inch frame higher in the bed. He was so tall he had scooted down to the bottom. I thanked God for letting me minister to him in this physical way again.

The nurse left. I remained and said a quick prayer to my Father: "God, don't let me blow it this time. Help me to say what he needs to hear to accept and believe in You."

This time I said what God wanted said in the beginning. This time I knew my puny human love was not going to accomplish anything. He needed God's love!

He cried and listened. He couldn't talk, but I knew he felt God's love in that intensive care unit. I felt God's love flow out of me. I held him and let him cry. I told him I would see him again. I prayed over him and left him looking very peaceful.

He died two days later. I know I will see him again. I have no doubt he is with the Lord Jesus Christ in paradise. My heart shouted out, *Thanks, God, for second chances!*

We are put here on earth to build treasure into people, not into our bank accounts. We are to deposit God into as many people as He brings into our lives. Think about it. There is not going to be any human-made things going on ahead of you into heaven—only the treasure you deposit into the lives of others. Don't go in empty-handed. People are our treasures.

Thank You for giving me a second chance, Lord
Jesus. Praise You that heaven has another member
in the family of God. Amen.

Hypocrite Housewife

Woe to you, scribes and Pharisees, hypocrites! For
you cleanse the outside of the cup and dish, but
inside they are full of extortion and self-indulgence.
Blind Pharisee, first cleanse the inside of the cup
and dish, that the outside of them may be clean also.
—Matthew 23:25–27 (NKJV)

I read these verses and got a good chuckle, not because of the lack of seriousness of the facts the Lord Jesus stated, but because of my weekend. My family was coming over for a resurrection celebration on Sunday. I had worked four double shifts and quite a few single shifts in the past two weeks at the hospital. I had to get my house in order.

I switched days with another person and got Saturday off. I tore into the house. Stuff went under things. Things went on top of things. Things got shoved into the already disastrous basement. Surfaces were cleaned. Visible surfaces were straightened, vacuumed, and mopped. Woohoo! It looked presentable, but underneath it all, I knew things were not really clean.

On the surface, my house looked good, smelled good (due to my candles and sprays), felt good because my family was there, and sounded good because of all the laughter and family chatter. But alas, I am a hypocrite housewife.

Take a look at your life, your physical house. Does it look good on the surface because of your designer clothing but is filthy in the Lord's sight? Does it smell good because of your expensive colognes and perfumes, but to the Lord, you stink to high heaven because of the filth you keep hidden where only He can smell it? Do you mouth things that sound good but go no deeper than the shallow heart that speaks them? Do you laugh when your heart is crying out for meaning?

Stop shoving things way down deep; God sees them anyway. Quit cleaning the outside, and let God cleanse you through and through. Quit trying to straighten out your own life, being greedy and self-indulgent. Underneath it all you, God know things are not right. Let the Father really cleanse you.

Wash me thoroughly from my iniquity, And cleanse me from my sin. (Psalm 51:2 NKJV)

> Lord, help me not to be a hypocrite Christian.
> Clean me and purge me from what I want to keep
> hidden from people because You see it anyway.
> Help me, Lord, to be real with You, and may it
> become part of what the rest of the world sees.
> Amen.

Growing Older

Cast me not off in the time of old age; forsake me
not when my strength faileth.

—Psalm 71:9 (KJV)

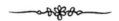

I met Kay, the most amazing Italian woman. When I met her, she was
ninety-two years young.

She is an avid reader and keeps her mind keen with much use.
She lives alone and tries to take a walk when weather permits. She
was the perfect host and wouldn't let us serve ourselves but insisted
on serving us.

Through the years, Kay had quite a bout with cancer. She won!
She has been totally bald for the past twenty-five years, is minus her
breasts and most of her lymph nodes, and has had massive thyroid
surgery. But she is alive and mentally more acute than most young
people.

She had quite a story to tell. She was married at age fifteen, and her
mother feared she was going to be an old maid because her sister had
married at age thirteen. After being married for a while and having no
babies, they decided to adopt from the local orphanage. They found
a beautiful, three-year-old Italian girl and named her Mary Kay. Kay
poured her love and life into this beautiful girl. Mary Kay married and
had two children of her own, Joanna and Anthony.

Pain came to Kay in the form of death. She lost her husband of
seventy-five years, and six months later, she lost her beautiful Mary
Kay to cancer. She questioned the "Master," as she calls Him, about

why He didn't take her. He quietly told her she was needed for the young ones.

As I looked at this beautiful lady who is many years my senior, I realized she views me as a "young one." Her life is now centered on staying alive for her grandchildren and making them journals and family albums to preserve their heritage. She stays active and alive at age ninety-two! What a lesson to me. What a lesson for all of us! We are never too old to be useful to the Master. Never!

Kay's strength is failing, but her Master is there for her every step of the way. As I left, she hugged me. I will always remember the sparkle in her eyes as she told me, "The Devil doesn't want me, and God won't take me, so I must still have a purpose to serve."

Lord, may I age with the grace, hope, and the
excellent attitude my friend Kay has. Thank You for
letting me see her vibrant life even at age ninety-
two. Amen.

Consider the Lilies

Consider the lilies how they grow: they toil not,
they spin not; and yet I say unto you, that Solomon
in all his glory was not arrayed like one of these.
—Luke 12:27 (KJV)

I had a beautiful rhododendron bush in my front yard. My daughter, Cristi, and her cousins decided to give me a gift. They pulled all the young flowers off the bush and gave them to me. Because the flowers were picked while in their prime, my rhododendron bush suffered and did not bear flowers again for many years. They certainly did not consider the flowers and how they grew.

The chapter-opening verse is a simple yet profound lesson from the Lord. "Consider the lilies how they grow." Notice it does not say where they grow, when they grow, or why they grow. It says, "how they grow." The Lord Jesus chooses how they grow. He created them. He waters and nourishes them. He picks their colors. He gives them fragrance. They live and die at His bidding.

Are you growing how the Lord desires you to grow? He created you. Be watered and nourished by the Word of God. No matter what your color or looks, be satisfied with who He made you to be. Leave a fragrance of Christ in the world, not your own fragrance. Be content to live for Him and die at His bidding.

Just as the lilies, we will mature and grow into old age, die, and seed the way for others. Or we will be cut down in our prime. This is the Lord's choice because He planted us on this earth. If we die and pave the way by leaving good seeds, this brings a bumper crop for the kingdom. If we are cut down in our prime, God will give our lives meaning and purpose.

Quit toiling and spinning. Let God tell you how you should grow. You are clothed in His righteousness.

Lord, thank You for creating me exactly as I am.
Thank You for Your righteousness. Help me to grow
in You by the washing of the water of Your Word.
May the fragrance of my life be a sweet perfume to
You as I live out my days. Amen.

Angels We Have Heard on High

And suddenly there was with the angel a multitude
of the heavenly host praising God and saying:
"Glory to God in the highest, And on earth peace,
goodwill toward men!"
—Luke 2:13–14 (NKJV)

There is a saying among people that I can truly identify with as a mother of five: "Put on your big boy/girl pants, and deal with it!"

I was sitting in service the Sunday before Christmas and the carol "Angels We Have Heard on High" rang out from the congregation. For no apparent reason to all onlookers, I began to cry. These were not tears of sadness but tears of deep memory, thanksgiving, and blessing.

Many years ago we attended a Christmas Day service. All families were encouraged to be part of the service with songs, music, poems, readings, or testimonies of what the Lord had done for them in the past year. Our family, being of Mexican heritage, decided to sing the carol "Angels We Have Heard on High" in Spanish.

We practiced our words, and on Christmas Day went to worship Christ. When it was our time to sing, we went up front and began to sing with all our hearts. All of a sudden I remembered my youngest son was just beginning to be potty trained, and I had put big boy pants on him instead of a diaper. What if all the excitement got to him, and we were all embarrassed right in front of the entire congregation?

I looked out at all the familiar faces and realized if this unfortunate occurrence did happen, these people were my spiritual family. They stand on the sidelines, cheering me on when it's my turn to worship the Lord. I rested in the love of my brothers and sisters. We finished the song with no mishaps, but the story is told around the table at Christmas when we all get together.

If you feel like worshipping the Lord in your own special way anytime during the year and are afraid you might mess up, "Put on your big boy/girl pants, and deal with it!" Your brothers and sisters are as human as you, and they love you.

> Thank You, Lord, that You came to earth and put
> on skin so You could totally identify with us in our
> needs. Thank You for becoming like us so we could
> become like You. Amen.

Mountains and Old Age

There on the mountain that you have climbed you
will die and be gathered to your people.
—Deuteronomy 32:50 (NIV)

Even to your old age and gray hairs I Am He, I Am
He who will sustain you. I have made you and I will
carry you; I will sustain you and I will rescue you.
—Isaiah 46:4 (NIV)

In one of my favorite places in the world, Acadia, Maine, is a mountain named the Precipice. It is the most dangerous mountain to climb. People have fallen to their death on the climb. I have climbed that mountain!

As you climb the trail, you encounter a boulder field that can't be rushed through. You carefully climb from boulder to boulder. It is painstaking, and I thought more than once about quitting and descending to comfort and safety.

After the boulder field is a steady climb. Your legs and lungs threaten to give up on you. Just when you think it can't get any harder, it does.

Rungs and ladders were pounded into the rock face of the mountain, and you begin a vertical climb. With each hand over hand and rung by rung, you feel certain you are going to fall backward onto the rocks and trees below.

Next are small ledges that look down on sheer height and beauty. I carefully pressed my back to the rock face and inched my way along. May I add the ledges have no barriers to keep you from falling? May I also say if you are afraid of heights, this is no place to be? Park rangers have had to rescue people from here.

The last leg of the climb is just plain old torture. You are close enough to get excited but too far up to decide to quit. You're almost there!

Is God in all this? You bet He is! After God allowed Moses to see the Promised Land, He told Moses, "There on the mountain that you have climbed you will die and be gathered to your people." Moses was 120 years old at the time (Deuteronomy 34:7).

You see, when I got to the top of the Precipice, there was such an exhilaration and fulfillment I knew the climb was worth every painful step and every beautiful view. I stood victorious on the top and surveyed a panoramic view that is the most awesome thing in the world.

To me, life and old age are like that mountain. Life has boulder fields of struggle; I have encountered them. When I think life can't get any harder, it does. I have my back to the wall of life and find myself on ledges so fearful I don't dare look back. I just inch forward.

I get near the end of life, and it is sheer torture because I am close enough to death to become both excited and fearful. I can't quit because I am almost there.

Throughout all this life climb, my God has been there! He has sustained me, He has carried me, and He has rescued me. I have never been alone on this life's climb.

My faith tells me that when I get to the top of the mountain of life and die there, I'll survey a panoramic, heavenly view that will be the most awesome thing not in this world but in all eternity. At the top of my mountain of life is the Promised Land.

On a purely human note, 120 years old sounds good!

> Thank You, Lord Jesus, for going every step of
> the way up this mountain of life—even to old
> age—with me. I know You are with me. I feel Your
> awesome presence with me all the time. Amen.

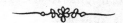

Taste and See

O taste and see that the Lord is good:
—Psalm 34:8 (KJV)

I asked the Lord straightforwardly, "How can I taste You, Lord, and how can I see You? This verse makes no sense to me. I'm not a cannibal; I can't taste You. You are Spirit, so I can't see You. What do You mean, "taste and see that the Lord is good"? The Lord is always ready to answer my childish questions. He answered this one, also.

He took me back in my mind to a day when I was having a picnic on the rocks along the rugged coastline of Maine. I was eating the most delicious homemade bread. I bought it fresh and hot, straight out of a local bakery's oven. I had huge hunks of corned beef, a crisp dill pickle, sharp New York cheddar cheese, and my favorite fruit of the vine. My taste buds were having a feast. This was good!

I looked out over the roaring Atlantic Ocean, enjoying the beauty before me. I could see for miles and miles. Seagulls mulled around me, hoping for a taste of my lunch. I could see them up close and beautiful. I could see the waves crashing against the rocks in all their fury and splendor. They ruled the shoreline. Oh, this was so good!

I took a deep, contented breath. I could taste the salt air on my tongue. The wind ruffled my hair with a cool Atlantic breeze. The sun was warm on my face. I could see the beauty of the Lord's creation all around me.

That's it! Wow, Lord, way cool.

Who created the wheat that makes my bread? Who created the steer that makes my corned beef? Who created the cucumbers that make my dill pickles? Who created the grapes that made the fruit of the vine? Who made the cow that produces my cheese? The Lord created all these things to give me the pleasure of taste.

Who created the ocean? Who created the seagulls? Who put the salt in the ocean spray? Who created the wind? Who created the sun? Who created the rocks to stop the oceans? Who caused the waves to crash and rule the shoreline? The Lord created these things for me to see.

Every created thing I taste and every created thing I see is a gift from the Lord, who is so good to create all these things for my pleasure. Why did He do it? Because He is so good! Today, taste and see that the Lord is good.

Thank You, Lord, for the beauty You have created
all around just for the pleasure it brought You to
create them for humankind. Amen.

Busybody

But let none of you suffer as a murderer, a thief, an evildoer, or as a busybody in other people's matters.
—1 Peter 4:15–16 (NKJV)

After a while, my job in the behavioral health-care unit became physically more than I could handle. I went to work at an assisted-living facility.

A father/son maintenance team worked at this facility. The father was very jovial, easygoing, and always ready to dispense his maintenance duties with a smile. His son was a very sullen, quiet, despondent person. I formed an opinion of him that was not very favorable.

One day I was in the breakroom for lunch at the same time the father was having lunch. His son missed work that day. I asked how his son was doing—after forming my own opinion, of course.

He said "Well, he's doing better."

"What do you mean, 'better'?" He told me his son lost his young wife to cancer about a year before. She had worked in the dietary area in this facility. They were married only one year, and his son was having a very hard time adjusting.

I read the chapter-opening verse, and it struck me how quickly I can form opinions of other people. I sometimes even pass these opinions on without an iota of information about why the person is the way he or she is.

Everyone has a story. We are not all privileged to know that story if not a close friend. I let this verse wash over my soul. Do you see where a busybody is placed in God's Word? Right up there with murderer, thief, and evildoer.

> Lord, forgive me for being a busybody and forming
> opinions of others without accurate information
> and certainly without compassion. Amen.

Red Sky

Then the Pharisees and Sadducees came, and
testing Him asked that He would show them
a sign from heaven. He answered and said to
them, "When it is evening you say, 'It will be fair
weather, for the sky is red'; and in the morning, 'It
will be foul weather today, for the sky is red and
threatening.' Hypocrites! You know how to discern
the face of the sky, but you cannot discern the signs
of the times. A wicked and adulterous generation
seeks after a sign, and no sign shall be given to it
except the sign of the prophet Jonah." And He left
them and departed.
—Matthew 16:1–4 (NKJV)

It had been raining, cold, windy, and dark for a few days. As I went to work on Sunday, the day came with a beautiful, red sky. It promised to be a beautiful, sunny day. I drove to work due east, so I got to enjoy the magnificence of the sunrise. The spectacular sunrise produced an awe in my heart and soul by the time I arrived at work.

When I entered work, the nightshift was waiting to go home. I said, "Did you see the beautiful sunrise today? God is awesome to give us this promise of life going on for another day, isn't He?" All I got was a grumble and a nod.

One of the elderly residents heard my words. She walked over to the huge picture windows that face east and said, "Look at that sunrise. Look at the clouds. They are tipped with red, like mountains rising up!"

She went over to some other elderly residents who were waiting for breakfast and remarked to them about the sunrise. I watched that elderly woman for the rest of the day as she came and went. She was encouraged and uplifted by the beauty of God's sunrise.

What greater sign from heaven can we get from the Father than the beauty of the sunrise, faithfully obeying His voice, coming up at the prescribed time in the morning with its promise of a new day and continued life?

> The Heavens declare the glory of God: and the firmament shows His handiwork. Day unto day utters speech, and night unto night reveals knowledge there is no speech nor language where their voice is not heard. (Psalm 19:1–3 NKJV)

Father God, I thank You that Your creation speaks without a word or a voice, and yet it shouts Your glory. Amen.

Goodness and Mercy

Surely goodness and mercy shall follow me all the
days of my life: and I will dwell in the house of the
Lord forever.
—Psalm 23:6 (NKJV)

I have a special memory of my last pastor. He has gone to be with the
Lord now. He was a sparkly, blue-eyed Scotsman with snow-white
hair. He was like a father to me. He was gentle, kind, loving, and never
harsh with anyone.

He told a story of when he was in Scotland and watching a
shepherd guard his flock. The shepherd had two old sheepdogs he'd
named Goodness and Mercy. He said he watched as Goodness and
Mercy kept the sheep in line and safe from harm's way.

Goodness and Mercy gently guided the sheep away from the edge
of a dangerous overlook and back to the flock. He said Goodness and
Mercy kept a close eye on the sheep, all the while listening to the
shepherd and what he told them to do.

He related that at the end of the day, Goodness and Mercy would
go in big circles around the sheep, getting them closer and closer until
they were in a small huddle. Goodness and Mercy then guided them
into the sheepfold for the night.

After all the sheep were safe in the fold, Goodness and Mercy sat
at the feet of the shepherd, and he told them in his Scottish brogue,
"Ey, ye did a good job today. I'm proud o' you. I could no ha'e done
it without ye." Goodness and Mercy were totally satisfied with their
shepherd's loving approval.

My pastor then said,

> This was a great lesson to me. It taught me that I
> am to guide the sheep of the Great Shepherd's flock
> with goodness and mercy at all times. Goodness
> and mercy will win out every time. I am to steer
> them away from harm and keep them in the right
> paths, but always with goodness and mercy. I also
> realized He is the Great Shepherd; I am a sheepdog
> that does the bidding of the Great Shepherd.

At the end of my life, I want to go out in a blaze of glory and sit
at the feet of my Great Shepherd and hear Him say, "Ey son, Ye did a
good job today. I'm proud o' you. I could no ha'e done it without ye."

> Thank You, Father God, for sending human pastors
> into my life that have led me with the goodness
> and mercy they have received from You. Thank
> You for keeping them faithful to do Your will and
> Your work on this earth to expand the kingdom of
> heaven. Amen.

Loved Ones Bury You

Then Abraham gave up the ghost, and died in a
good old age, an old man, and full of years; and
was gathered to his people. And his sons Isaac and
Ishmael buried him in the cave of Machpelah.
—Genesis 25:8 (KJV)

And Isaac gave up the ghost, and died, and was
gathered unto his people, being old and full of days:
and his sons Esau and Jacob buried him.
—Genesis 35:29 (KJV)

It is ironic that Isaac and Ishmael were of different mothers and had different beliefs, but when it came time to bury their father, Abraham, they put aside differences and performed their honor to the memory of their father by being unified for the time at hand. Abraham went to be with his God.

It is equally ironic that Jacob and Esau were twins, but their differences of opinion and diversity of beliefs had kept them apart for most of their adult lives. But when it came time to bury their father, Isaac, they came together as brothers and honored the memory of their father. Isaac went to be with his God.

We could take lessons from these men of the Bible. Death is no time to bring up differences of opinion, diversities of beliefs, or even rights to possessions or parentage preferences. Death is a time to honor the life of the deceased. Death is a time to bring to heart and mind the good memories of that person. Death is a time for unity, not division.

This type of remembering brings honor and respect to the deceased. Even more, it brings honor, respect, and dignity to us all as well as to the God who gave us our lives in the first place. We can gently release that loved one to be with God.

Words said in time of extreme emotion are more often than not said in a second but left to hurt painfully for a lifetime. Be silent at the death of a loved one except to give praise, honor, and good memories to the deceased. You will never have need to regret your words if you do this.

> Lord Jesus, please restrain my words in times of
> deepest grief, and put a watch over my mouth so I
> do not dishonor my Lord, my God, or the memory
> of the one who is stepping into Your presence.
> Amen.

The Small Gate

Enter through the narrow gate. For wide is the gate
and broad is the road that leads to destruction, and
many enter through it. But small is the gate and
narrow the road that leads to life, and only a few
find it.
—Matthew 7:13–14 (NIV)

I attended a young Christian's funeral yesterday. I listened very carefully to what all the people had to say. Although my friend was a tall man, his friends told of how he was small enough to love little children. I heard how my friend had chosen to go to Bible college to serve His God and then did that very thing immediately. I heard how he gave of his time, talents, and his heart to the work of God's kingdom. I listened to story after story of a man who was small in his eyes but big in the work of God.

I began searching my heart and soul. Am I missing that "small gate" that leads to eternal life? Looking down at that young, handsome face, I had to reassess my profession of belief in a holy God. I looked forward and saw the opening to that small gate. I saw how big I am in my eyes. I realized I was much too big to fit through that gate.

The Lord Jesus said, "only a few find it." The Lord Jesus is truth. He cannot lie, so I must believe this. Jesus helped me find the gate, so I know it's possible to go through it. I realized to go through the small gate I must decrease much more than I think I already have. My Lord must increase in my life much more than I have allowed in the past. John 30:3 (KJV) reads, "He must increase, but I must decrease."

When will the Lord Jesus say to me, "Come"? When I am small enough to fit through that gate, I'll hear the welcome voice of my Lord

Jesus Christ say, "Come, you who are blessed by my Father, take your inheritance, the Kingdom prepared for you since the creation of the world" (Matthew 25:34 NIV).

> Help me to decrease in my own estimation and
> allow the Holy Spirit to increase my Lord and
> Savior until I totally disappear into eternity. Amen.

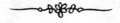

The Small Gate Home

For wide is the gate and broad is the road that leads
to destruction, and many enter through it. But
small is the gate and narrow the road that leads to
life, and only a few find it.
—Matthew 7:13-14 (NIV)

I am the gate; whoever enters through me will be
saved.
—John 10:9 (NIV)

Suppose one of you has a hundred sheep and loses
one of them. Does he not leave the ninety-nine in
the open country and go after the lost sheep until
he finds it? And when he finds it, he joyfully puts it
on his shoulders and goes home?
—Luke 15:4–6 (NIV)

I hope someone out there can identify with this poem. I hope someone
out there can honestly say they have a difficult time with Christianity
at times, the many denominations, the total lack of adherence to the
church in the New Testament, and that your faith falters in times of
weakness. This poem isn't the constant feeling of my life. It is one of
those faltering days that it was written. But like the psalms of David,
by the end of it, the Lord was there waiting for me, just like He always
is. Praise His holy name!

I live in a world that is filled with pain.
There is hate and violence, and it is so insane.

There is fear and vice, crookedness and greed.
This madness moves forward, and I must concede
That the world has gone mad, so filled with hate.
So I search much harder for *that small gate*
That leads to God and His holy life.
But I keep tripping on the broad road filled with
strife.
I scramble back on the straight and narrow.
Next thing I know, I'm walking through sorrow.
I run to the church to find my way.
I search in there for a holy ray
To light my path and bear my load
As I struggle back on the narrow road.
And while I'm there, to one I called "friend"
I was praying some love he might extend,
Shoots me from the shadows and wounds my soul.
I feel I've been burned with a red-hot coal.
I realize many who think they're straight
And headed for that narrow gate
Are on that broad way that leads to hell.
So I pick myself up where I was shot and fell
And begin again to search for that way
That will lead me to God some bright day.
If it's not in the world, and it's not in the church,
Please tell me, God, where do I search?
If it's not in the church and not in the world,
Where is the gate that is made of pearl?
The one that is small and few there find
Must be in my spirit and not my mind.
So I cease all reason, knowledge, and thought.
Get back on the way that my Savior sought.
Keep my focus on His perfect life.
Set my face like flint on the afterlife.
Know He walked that narrow way

And shed His blood, so He might pay
A debt to God that was mine to own,
Was crucified and laid behind a stone,
Was raised to life on that third day,
Not just for me but all who stray.
He walked through that narrow gate,
Took His own blood and cleaned my slate,
Bore me on His shoulders at Calvary.
He will carry me home, where I'll forever be.
I did not find that gate, you see.
That gate is Jesus, and He found me. Amen.

Jesus Wept

Jesus wept.
Then Jesus said, "Did I not tell you that if you
believed, you would see the glory of God?"
"Lazarus, come out!"
"Take off the grave clothes and let him go."
—John 11:35, 40, 43–44 (NIV)

One of Jesus's good friends on earth had been dead for four days. The Lord knew he had died and also knew He would raise Lazarus to life again. Why did Jesus weep?

My mom died August 15, 2005. She believed in the Lord Jesus Christ. She is free from all suffering and pain. I feel a peace about her death. This morning, the floodgate of human tears burst forth. Why? My mom is much better off than anyone here on earth. I am at complete peace about her death. So why did I weep?

My spirit opened up, and I knew why I cry and why Jesus cried. When Adam and Eve ate the forbidden fruit, they brought death to the human race. Two created beings which had the image of God were now subject to death. Satan hates God. Now Satan has the right to bring death to every human being on the face of the earth. None of us are exempt.

Satan hates us because we bear the image of God. No matter how obscure, sullied, or faint it is, we all bear God's image. In the beginning, Satan set out to obliterate that image from us. He cannot because God placed it there!

Satan sends pain, cancer, diabetes, heart attacks, mental and physical impairments, distortions, mutations, birth defects, and every horrible thing he can to the human anatomy because he has the power to make us die. He wants our pain and suffering to keep us from believing. But God has the power to make us live forever. How? Just believe.

I believe Jesus wept because He could see all the pain and suffering humanity would have to bear on their way to death. I believe He wept because of those who would not believe and have eternal life. So I cried and cried until I thought my heart would burst from my chest cavity. I felt His pain, and I felt my pain.

Then, in the most beautiful thoughts, I was comforted. I thought of Jesus in glory, saying, "Eve Marie come forth." He gently tells the angels of God, "Take off the grave clothes, and let her go." Then He gently takes Mom into His arms and asks, "Did I not tell you that if you believed, you would see the glory of God?"

Bugeja, Eva Marie
Age eighty of Wyandotte, MI, born June 25, 1925–
passed away August 15, 2005.

My Mom

She carefully watches all that goes on in her
household and does not have to bear the
consequences of laziness.

—Proverbs 31:27 (NLT)

She could take a beat-up, old house and make it into a home. Orange crates, old pieces of fabric, and lye soap could transform the shabbiest farmhouse into a thing of beauty.

She could garden and preserve what she grew. She could sew, and she could read *Mother Goose*. Once she even raised and harvested earthworms for bait. She sold them beside the road to people going by on their way to fish.

Her children were dressed neatly and in clean, starched clothing even when she was wearing last year's hand-me-downs. She didn't wear makeup but was prettier than all her daughters. She only finished eighth grade but was intelligent and knew the Word of God well from her youth.

She got up in the morning and put on a pot of beans, got three loads of laundry done, cleaned the part of the house people weren't sleeping in, watered the garden, fed eight cats and three dogs, and remember she promised to make a slingshot for one of her kids. You woke up to bacon frying and fried potatoes and gravy.

She was the hardest-working woman I ever met. I admired her strength and her ingenuity in making a house a home. She had that childlike quality that made you smile and big, beautiful, blue eyes that alternated between sparkling impishness to deepest sadness, a sadness she would not share no matter how hard you tried. She just said, "I feel blue."

My mom! I am honored and proud to have had her for eighty years. The Lord decided He wanted her for His home, and this is my first Mothers Day without her here. But she is here in each blue eye, each childlike mannerism, each kid who loves to fish, each one of us who loves to work and make a house a home, and to each of us who have cracked our knuckles on a homemade slingshot. Thanks, Mom. You did really good, and I hope I'm just like you in all those excellent ways.

> Thank You, Father God, for putting me into the
> perfect home for my own purpose in Your larger
> scheme of life. Thank You for a mom who instilled
> many good qualities and habits into the lives of her
> children. Thank You, Father, for the eighty years
> You gave her on this earth and that heaven is now
> enjoying her. Amen.

Family

Then Joseph kissed each of his brothers and wept over them, and after that they began talking freely with him.
—Genesis 45:15 (NLT)

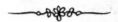

My mom's estate was finally settled two years after she died. She was not wealthy, but there was a small amount for each of us six siblings. We decided to take a riverboat trip in a southern state together in honor of our mom. She had said the best vacation she ever had was on a houseboat with her family. We took the trip on the anniversary of her death.

We all talked about Mom, remembering all the good things from our childhood. But I have to admit we were not in agreement on all things. Suddenly, one of Mom's favorite songs came on the radio, and one by one, we began to cry. We embraced each other in turn and clung to the moment for a while. That was a very freeing thing for me.

Just like Joseph and his brothers, after we wept together, embraced each other, and enjoyed the good and not the differences in opinions, we were able to talk freely. Satan lost a foothold. We are family, and love, weeping, and putting things behind us helped us to talk more freely with each other. It bound us closer as a family.

Lord Jesus, You know exactly how to bind us
together as a family. Please help people everywhere
to realize what a blessing it is to be placed in a
family. It is a double blessing when we are all part of
the family of God. Amen.

Mom's Vine

Therefore, since we are surrounded by such a huge crowd of witnesses to the life of faith, let us strip off every weight that slows us down, especially the sin that so easily trips us up. And let us run with endurance the race God has set before us.

—Hebrews 12:1 (NLT)

Ever since I was a small child, I watched my mom grow and love plants and flowers. Once she shoved a sweet potato into a jar of water and grew a sweet potato vine that reached all the way around her kitchen wall.

When she passed away, we were given the choice of what we wanted. I took a vine that sat on her dresser. I liked to imagine it was the first thing she saw each morning and the last thing she saw at night.

The week before my surgery, I decided because temperatures were in the high 60s and low 70s I'd carry all my houseplants up to the enclosed, unheated sundeck. I mistakenly believed spring was here to stay. Needless to say, Cleveland had snow, freezing temperatures, and very unspring weather while I was in the hospital.

When I came home, I looked out on the deck, and my heart sank. Most of my plants were black and drooping. They had frozen. Mom's vine was the only one that brought my heart real hurt. Some of the vines had reached fifteen to twenty feet when uncoiled. I had them arranged on a trellis to look like one massive vine tree.

When I felt a bit better, I decided to take pruning shears and cut back all the dead, black leaves of the vine in hope some small amount of life had survived in its roots. As I cut away the dead leaves, I remembered Mom. Great memories. Kid memories. My mom could grow anything, and I had let her vine die from human neglect.

As I cut away the last of the dead leaves, I saw a bit of green. A small vine had survived because the dead ones sheltered it from the freezing temperatures. So I started all over again with the vine, digging in the earth, giving plant food, and being thankful for the remaining life in the vine. The Lord whispered a parable lesson deep in my heart.

There is a huge crowd, including Mom, gone in death and leaving a heritage of faith that is mine. Their lives overshadow, define, and encourage who I am and how I have arrived at my faith. May those who have gone before me find me faithful.

Lord Jesus, thank You for all the teachers, mentors, friends, and family who have helped in this heritage of faith they have passed on to me. Their love and care overshadow me even now and encourage me to grow more in my faith. Amen.

PONDERINGS

And Mary kept all these things and pondered them
in her heart.

—Luke 2:19 (KJV)

"Pondering," by definition, is to think deeply, weigh mentally, and consider carefully a matter. "Meditate" is a common synonym for ponder.

Being the storyteller I am, I love it when the Lord Jesus gives me a clear spiritual/moral application in an everyday occurrence after I have pondered it in my heart.

The following ponderings, as I refer to them, are what I have received from my Lord and Savior in many aspects of life or living throughout my pilgrimage here on this earth.

Christmastime of Long Ago

I was eight years old on the last Christmas my dad was alive. Christmas was a huge celebration in our home. Dad made a big issue about finding just the right tree. It was decorated with patience and care. Each family member participated under Dad's guidance, placing each item on the tree exactly where he thought it looked best.

I lay under the tree, looking up at all the lights in awe. The pine smell of a Christmas tree still brings back memories of my dad.

The only time of year we had fresh tangerines was at Christmastime! It was Dad's special gift to us. I still associate tangerines with Christmas and sweet memories of the loving, giving man my dad was.

Dad played the Santa game with his children. By the time Christmas Day finally arrived, I was in high gear, and nothing could quell my excitement in getting up to see what Santa placed under the tree just for me.

The following poem was written from the memories in the heart of a very happy little girl.

Country Christmas

Christmastime of long ago,
As pure as the driven snow.
When love was all we really had,
The children and Mom and Dad,
An old farmhouse upon the hill,
A pot-bellied stove to stop the chill.
Big, comfy beds with homemade quilts,

An old front porch that sat on stilts.
The tree! The best we'd ever had!
Cut from the woods by our own dad.
We all piled in that old black truck,
Chains on the wheels so we didn't get stuck.
Away to Grandma's house we'd go,
Fighting excitement, cold, and snow.
There were aunts, uncles, and many cousins,
Sweets and goodies by the dozens.
We had chicken frying in the pan,
Jams and jellies in the can.
There were Christmas carols in the air,
Sung from our hearts just like a prayer.
We'd eat and laugh and sing and play,
And talk of Santa and Christmas Day.
Those times were precious to my heart,
And the memories remain a part
Of Christmastime and all its glory
As I pass along my precious story.
The Lord has taken Mom and Dad.
At Christmastime my soul is sad.
Until I stop and realize
We'll be together by and by.
Christmastime's not quite the same.
No Mom or Dad for Santa's game.
But memories flood through my mind,
The special, precious, childlike kind.
And I give thanks to God above
for sending down His Son of love.
And now I have a different Dad,
The greatest one I've ever had.
There is no present beneath His tree;
His present hung on Calvary.

Little Child

Whosoever therefore shall humble himself as this
little child, the same is great in the kingdom of
heaven.

—Matthew 18:4 (KJV)

Little children are open, honest, and very naïve and accepting of what
is taught to them. They possess a humility that is rare in adults. It
displays itself in submissiveness and obedience to parents. I most
certainly was that at age eight, when my dad died.

Mom was twenty-eight when Dad died. She was almost a child
herself as she took on the responsibility of raising three little girls all
alone. In her childlike thinking, she decided to be totally honest with
us. She told us things would be changing, and we were not to expect
life to remain the same. Things indeed were never the same again.

The first holiday after Dad's death was Easter Sunday. I had just
turned nine years old. Mom told us right away there would be no
Easter baskets because there was no Easter bunny. She went on to say
there was no Santa, either. She went further and stated quite bluntly
there was no tooth fairy; Dad slipped the money under our pillows.

My older sister was not surprised by this revelation, being three
years older than I. She didn't believe the myths anymore. My younger
sister was too young to even know what the myths were.

I was always a quiet child, so no one knew at the time how
much this disclosure devastated me. My dad was taken away, and
now the Easter bunny, Santa, and the tooth fairy were taken away.
My childhood trust and expectations ended pretty much that day.
Enjoyment of holiday celebrations ended with Dad's death.

I write this only to relay why I decided not to teach my children lies about any mythical character. A lie is a lie, and we dare not call it the truth. That game of myths devastated a little one.

My husband and I have taken flak for our decision, but I have never been sorry for being truthful with my children about holiday myths. Christmas is to celebrate the birth of our Savior. Easter Sunday is to celebrate the resurrection of our Savior. There were gifts under the tree from Mom and Dad. There was an Easter basket full of goodies from Mom and Dad. My children knew who gave them their gifts.

When a tooth was lost, the game was to place the coin for the lost tooth under the pillow without the child waking up and discovering Mom or Dad placing it there. If the child caught the parent, twice the amount was given for the lost tooth.

I never felt my children lost out on any childhood enjoyment because of our choice to teach them the truth about holidays. If you teach your children when young the lie of a nonexistent Santa, Easter bunny, and tooth fairy they cannot see and they discover the truth when older, doesn't it make sense they may think you lied about a God they cannot see at that older age also?

Lord Jesus, You are the truth. You are the only
truth in a liars' world. May we as parents be very
honest in what we teach the malleable minds of the
children you entrusted to us. Amen.

The Handkerchief

And he, stooping down and looking in, saw the
linen cloths lying there; yet he did not go in. Then
Simon Peter came, following him, and went into
the tomb; and he saw the linen cloths lying there,
and the handkerchief that had been around His
head, not lying with the linen cloths, but folded
together in a place by itself. Then the other disciple,
who came to the tomb first, went in also; and he
saw and believed.

—John 20:5–8 (NKJV)

It was Christmas 1957, and I was feeling sorry for myself. Mom had collected us three girls from our foster homes in three states. It had just been four short months since I was in a home where there were Christmas presents, a Christmas tree, heat, and lights.

I remembered Christmases when my dad was alive. Having selective memory and not reality memory, all I could think of was the tree, the presents, the food, and the warmth of family, not to mention the warmth of my house.

There were no presents for me or my older sister that year. We decided that since our youngest sister still believed in Santa, we would forgo our presents, so she could keep her childhood belief in Santa.

The tree was a free tree. It had handmade ornaments and strings of popcorn. As long as we had coal for the furnace and remembered to stoke it, we had heat to some degree.

A girl from across the street, a few years younger than I, knocked on the door. She had a tiny box in her hand. It was a handkerchief with a tiny flower embroidered in the corner. She could not contain her excitement. It was the first Christmas present she had ever received. Her parents had purchased it for her.

I looked at the handkerchief and thought, *It couldn't have cost more than nineteen cents. What is she so excited about?* I looked closer and saw she had tears in her eyes. I felt like the biggest jerk in history. Her gratitude was enormous, and mine was nonexistent.

I thought about this story many times over the years. I thought of my ingratitude toward God. When I read this version of Scripture and saw that word *handkerchief*, that story immediately came into my heart. Not for any other reason than this New King James Version called the headpiece that covered the Lord's head a handkerchief. It was because of this folded handkerchief that the apostle John believed Jesus had been resurrected.

My whole attitude changed that Christmas Day because of a handkerchief. Isn't that what Christmas is all about? A babe was born to die, but He was resurrected.

> For God so loved the world that He gave His only
> begotten Son, that whoever believes in Him should
> not perish but have everlasting life. (John 3:16
> NKJV)

I vowed that if I married and had children, I would teach them about God, the true gift-giver. Everlasting life is the only gift worth having any Christmas season. It cost God everything and the recipients nothing.

Holy Trinity

For I determined not to know any thing among
you, save Jesus Christ, and Him crucified.
—1 Corinthians 2:2 (KJV)

I taught my first Sunday school class when I was eighteen. I taught six- to eight-year-olds. About three months into my teaching, I chose as a topic the doctrine of the Holy Trinity. Many seasoned scholars dare not try to explain it, and they can't.

I studied and thought I had a pretty good grasp on the subject. As I tried to explain it to my wide-eyed class, a little boy asked me, "How can one person be three people?" Kids! They are the hardest ones to teach because their questions are genuine, extremely hard, and really good.

I was ready for this question. I had come up with a little poem to explain such a question. I said with conviction, "Three in One, One in Three, The One in the middle died for me! Father, Son, and Holy Spirit." Then I had them repeat it.

I asked, "Do you understand?" All the little heads bobbed up and down but one. This little guy just looked at me blankly and shook his head. I told him to learn the poem and come back and repeat it to me. He was a good boy and did just that. He repeated it to me quite a few Sundays in a row. I didn't dare ask him if he understood. I just asked him to learn it.

Twenty years, three states, and four children later, I was invited to the twenty-fifth anniversary of this church. I went with excitement to see all the people I hadn't seen in years. I saw a very handsome young man with a baby on his hip and one hanging onto his leg. He asked, "Mrs. Ramirez, you don't remember me, do you?" I had to admit I didn't. He looked me in the eye and said, "Three in One, One in Three, The One in the middle died for me, Father, Son, and Holy Spirit. I still don't understand it, but I believe it and teach it to my kids."

I think back at how ridiculous I was to try to teach such a deep theological subject to children. Jesus loves them, and He loves me. He is full of grace toward us all.

> I Thank You, One in the middle who died for me! I
> still don't understand the concept of the Trinity. I
> just know it is absolutely true, and I'm teaching it to
> all my kids.

Faith and Good Works

This is a faithful saying, and these things I want you
to affirm constantly, that those who have believed
in God should be careful to maintain good works.
These things are good and profitable to men.
—Titus 3:8 (NKJV)

What does it profit, my brethren, if someone says
he has faith but does not have works? Can faith save
him? If a brother or sister is naked and destitute of
daily food, and one of you says to them, "Depart in
peace, be warmed and filled," but you do not give
them the things which are needed for the body,
what does it profit? Thus also faith by itself, if it
does not have works, is dead.
—James 2:14–18 (NKJV)

She was a new Christian. She was very poor. Her family needed food,
and she asked the church for help. They told her they would pray for
her needs. She answered quite simply and honestly, "I'd rather have
a hot dog."

This is a perfect example of faith without works. Read what Paul
says in the book of Titus. Good works are good and profitable for
humankind. The good part is faith; the profitable part is works. Can
it be any simpler than that?

Look at the book of James. He is also quite clear. There is no profit if you just have faith. Faith is an inward thing. The proof of faith bubbles out and becomes an outward action. Works! If there is no bubbling out, there is no inward belief. Your faith is dead. If your faith is alive, it bubbles out and is profitable to humankind.

If someone asks you for clothing and food and you piously answer, "Depart in peace, be warmed and filled," where is your bubbling, thankful, merciful, loving spirit? You should possess one if the Holy Spirit has given you faith. Does your mouth say you have faith and your actions deny this?

What about this profit Titus and James speaks of? It is profit for the kingdom of God. It isn't your food, clothing, or money that God desires. It is profit of souls for His kingdom. How else can you gain profit on God's gift of faith except to invest it in humankind. It is our entire job on earth to worship and glorify Him and win souls into the kingdom of God.

You cannot speak to them of spiritual things until their physical needs are met. They do not yet know of spiritual things. Give them food, clothing, and love and then they can understand what working faith is. Offer them a dead faith, and they will reject Jesus Christ. Is your faith dead or alive?

Need Healing?

Who forgiveth all thine iniquities; who healeth all
thy diseases;
—Psalm 103:3 (KJV)

He healeth the broken in heart, and bindeth up
their wounds.
—Psalm 147:3 (KJV)

For this people's heart is waxed gross, and their ears
are dull of hearing, and their eyes they have closed;
lest at any time they should see with their eyes, and
hear with their ears, and should understand with
their heart, and should be converted, and I should
heal them.
—Matthew 13:15 (KJV)

I was hurt deeply. The wound went into my heart and soul and began
to cause physical symptoms. I had migraine headaches. My blood
sugar went so low I began to sleep seventeen to eighteen hours a day.
My thyroid was affected by the blood-sugar levels. I was depressed.
Why? Because someone had hurt me deeply, and I refused to let go of
the bitterness, hatred, and hurt.

My sin was lack of forgiveness. It caused true physical illnesses—
migraine headaches, hypoglycemia, underactive thyroid, and

clinical depression. My attitude affected my physical health in a very negative way.

I decided to believe the chapter-opening verses. I could be healed. The beginning step was to forgive the person who hurt me. The individual refused my offer of forgiveness. The Lord said He would heal me; He didn't say the other person was my business. I prayed for that person and stopped thinking negative thoughts about the individual. I refused to lie on my bed and think up scenarios of action against the person.

I began to heal. The first thing to go was the migraine headaches, which stopped when I stopped having negative thoughts. I began to eat a proper, high-protein diet, and my blood-sugar levels improved. The thyroid followed and became well because my insulin levels were corrected naturally. My new attitude took the depression away.

How did this all happen? I believed the Lord's Word. He heals the brokenhearted and binds their wounds. We often inflict those wounds on ourselves with our iniquities and sins of lack of forgiveness and hatred, a relationship we refuse to give up, a sinful habit, or other sins we cling to.

This healing takes time, but the first step is to truly desire healing from God. Then accept His cure. Do you need healing and an attitude change today? The Lord is in the body and mind healing business!

God's Tree

The righteous shall flourish like the palm-tree: He
shall grow like a cedar in Lebanon.
They are planted in the house of Jehovah; They
shall flourish in the courts of our God.
They shall still bring forth fruit in old age; They
shall be full of sap and green.
—Psalm 92:12–14 (ASV)

A huge maple tree grew in front of our home. It was huge when we moved into our home in 1974, towering about seventy-five feet tall. It has sustained a lot of damage during years of life. A car smashed into it and ripped off large portions of bark. I thought it would die. It did not. The wind tore large branches off throughout the years. One of those did massive amounts of damage to one of our cars. Still the tree lives on.

I can't give in to having it cut down. It houses families of squirrels. It is host to many nesting birds. One time it was a nest for honeybees. It shades my home and keeps it cool in the summer. I sit on my porch and enjoy the rustling of praise it gives to God when the wind blows.

The tree will have to come down soon. It has very few branches. Its roots have pulled up from the ground, and the tree is getting gnarled and less solid every season. Still, I love that tree. It produces beauty in springtime, awesome color in fall, and rest and shade for all in summer. In winter it wears a gown of snow-white branches lifted high in praise to the One who created it.

That tree is like us. The outside suffers the ravages of time, but on the inside, we are full of Holy Spirit sap that flows freely through our being with life. Even in old age we have much to give. The outside may suffer the effects of aging, but the inside grows younger and younger every day! When we are "young enough" in the Lord, we, too, will be transplanted in the court of our God.

Thank You, God, that You find us useful for Your work all the way to the end of our lives. Amen.

Corn Moon

God made two great lights—the greater light to
govern the day and the lesser light to govern the
night. He also made the stars.
—Genesis 1:16–17 (NIV)

The city does not need the sun or the moon to shine
on it, for the glory of God gives it light, and the
Lamb is its lamp.
—Revelation 21:23 (NIV)

I was wide-awake at 3:30 a.m. My mind raced, and my emotions were
raw. I got out of bed and made my way out the patio doors to the
second-floor porch. I leaned over the railing and let out a huge sigh.
My heart was heavy, and I couldn't determine why. I asked, "What's
wrong with me, Lord?"

Silence.

There was a warm summer breeze. The maple leaves rustled softly.
My wind chimes struck a quick melodious note. I heard a night owl
somewhere in the branches of the maple. The breeze ruffled my hair. I
smiled. I imagined the Lord ruffling my hair and smiling at me. Lord,
You are the only one I allow to ruffle my hair. My spirit lifted a bit.

I looked into the night sky. There was a huge corn moon looking
back down at me. It was beautiful! The breeze, the rustling leaves, the
melody of the wind chimes, the hooting of the night owl, and the full
corn moon were suddenly a miracle acknowledged deep in my spirit.

My mind remembered the Word. The Lord created and placed the sun in the sky to light and warm the earth He made for me. It ruled the day. He created and placed the moon in the sky to rule the night and control the tides and the cycle of woman and life.

Now there I was, looking into the night sky and being encouraged by the corn moon. God is still in the heavens. He is still in control. The sun still rises each morning and goes down each night. The moon is there every night, just as He promised.

I looked in awe at the miracle of the corn moon. The moon is there as a nightly promise, and I take its beauty and majesty for granted. Is it because I take God for granted? Do I cease to see His awesome provision for me every day?

The silence was gone. God spoke in a million voices in the beauty of the night. He spoke in the rustling maple leaves. He whispered in the breeze that ruffled my hair and made my wind chimes dance and sing. He cooed to me in the voice of the night owl. He peered down at me in the face of the full corn moon.

From Genesis to Revelation, the sun and moon stay their courses as they were commanded to do by their Creator. There is coming a cessation of time. The sun will disappear, and the moon will be no more. I won't need them.

God will be the glory greater than the sun, and Jesus will be the light that is more luminous than the moon. Until then, I have the miracle of His promise every day. I lift my face to the night sky, smile at the full corn moon, and breathe a prayer: "Thanks, God, I needed that."

Lesson from a Dandelion

(Published in *Mature Years* magazine, spring 2009)

I was working in my yard. Along with a pretty good sunburn, I also received a very neat lesson from God from, of all things, a dandelion.

I was pulling, yanking, and digging weeds out of my yard. I wondered, *Why don't we just have weed lawns instead of grass? It sure would help cut down on hours of back-breaking work!*

I thought I heard a giggle! It sort of sounded like a yellow giggle! You know, the way a dandelion would sound if it had a voice. I looked all around, and for the life of me, I couldn't figure out which dandelion had giggled. I peered into each and every face. Dandelions can keep a straight face, you know.

I returned to my tugging and pulling. Then all of a sudden, a soft summer breeze blew across the yard. All the little dandelion heads began to bob up and down in an almost prayer like dance. Some of the dandelions that were fluff ball seedlings (You know, those we used to pick as kids and blow with all our might to see if we could clear the stem with one puff, way back when we didn't know or care what weeds were?) began to float across the yard like tiny little helicopters, looking for a port to land on.

Suddenly, I felt my kid self rising to the surface. I love it when that happens! My heart wondered what had caused it. Kid memories; that's what caused it. I sat down right in the middle of the yard with a very unadultlike plop and began a conversation with my Abba.

"Abba, why did you make so many dandelions?" I asked.

"I like yellow," He replied.

"Well, yeah, I like yellow, too. It is one of my favorite colors. But they are such a nuisance," I bellyached.

Abba grinned a grin that makes His eyes light up and asked me, "Tell Me why you think they are a nuisance, little one?

I blurted out, "They grow wherever they want. They crowd out all the grass and spread like wildfire with those crazy puff seedlings."

He looked down, shook His head, and said, "They don't choose where to grow. I choose where I want them to grow, and they obey. They don't crowd out the grass. The grass is weaker and gives in to them. They spread their seedlings with the power of My breeze. They are not acting on their own, little one."

He gently continued. "You know, you could learn a lesson from the dandelion if you will. Why don't you always be obedient and go where I choose for you to go? Why don't you crowd out Satan's weaker growth by your hearty Holy Spirit power? Why don't you let your puff seedlings of love, joy, peace, patience, kindness, goodness, faithfulness, gentleness, and self-control spread around by the breath of My Holy Spirit and produce more for Me?"

I thought for a second of the deep truth spoken into my heart. I bowed my head like the dandelion and said, "Abba, I will try."

Abba said, "Don't worry, little one, I will help you. And by the way, you look beautiful in yellow."

Well, you know exactly what I did. I let out with a yellow dandelion giggle and said, "Abba, don't ever let me stop being a kid!"

Spring Peepers

For lo, the winter is past, The rain is over and
gone. The flowers appear on the earth; The time of
singing has come, and the voice of the turtledove is
heard in our land.

—Song 2:11–12 (NKJV)

There is a sound I remember from earliest childhood that has always
had a comforting effect on my soul. It is the sound of spring peepers.
Who can ignore a deafening chorus of spring peepers on a warm
spring night? These thumbnail-sized tree frogs leave their woodland
hibernation sites as early as March. Perched on grasses and sedges
at the edge of ponds or roadside ditches, the males call mates with
a shrill "Peep, peep, peep." Their brown or gray color, always with a
dark stripe on the sides of the head and dark markings on the back,
provide excellent camouflage against the dead spring grasses. If the
night is cold, peepers retreat under leaves and stems. You'll likely hear
hundreds before you ever see one.

I was on my way home in late March 1978 from visiting my sick
father-in-law. He was dying of cancer. I stopped at a roadside area to
rest. The sound that came to comfort my soul was that of the spring
peeper.

My father-in-law, Alejandro, died that year, but God sent us a son, Samuel Alejandro, eight months later. Besides his grandfather's name, he shares his love of music and his firm belief in God.

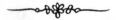

In March 1992, I was driving home from my mother-in-law's funeral. She had been killed in a car accident. I was alone with my children. I was so tired and weary of the personality clashes that occur at these types of functions. I had a four-hour drive ahead of me. I needed my husband, but he had to stay behind to take care of family business.

By the grace of God, I made it home. I stepped out of the vehicle and heard a chorus of spring peepers. Comfort and thanksgiving flooded my soul. I now remember her funeral as a beautiful tribute to a fine Christian lady.

In March 2006, I went to a birthday celebration of one of my favorite nephews. As I was driving the three and a half hours home, I labored over whether to stay in my job. I was anxious about continuing on in school at my age. I worried about the pain I saw on some of the faces at the party. I stopped for a sandwich and coffee.

I heard it for the first time this year! My comfort sound—spring peepers!

If God can comfort the heart with a spring peeper no larger than a human thumbnail, how much more can He comfort a person's heart with His mercy, love, and grace? I firmly left all aspects of the future in God's hands.

I hope there are spring peepers in heaven.

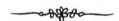

Daily Manna

Cause me to hear Your loving kindness in the
morning, For in You do I trust; Cause me to know
the way in which I should walk, For I lift up my soul
to You.

—Psalm 143:8 (NKJV)

We drove fifteen hours that night to get home. I was exhausted. I was hungry. I was discouraged. All I had to look forward to the next day was going back to a job I didn't particularly like.

The world is in a mess. Our armed services are in a war on terrorism I support but am tired of. There is a political race going on, and it is ugly to watch. There is sin and hate and greed in the world, and I just want to be home with the Lord.

I do not eat. I go to bed. I drop exhausted into a deep sleep. When I awake, I realize the sun is shining with brilliance only God can deliver. I go do what I do every morning of my life. I go to be with my Lord for a while before the day starts. My heart is very content. It is in the mornings that I feel His loving kindness the most. It is in the mornings I feel trust in Him the keenest.

Why? Because I am human, and I get tired, discouraged, and disheartened. It is in the morning, when I meet with my Lord, that I get the fuel I need for the day. His Word tells me what I need for that day. Like physical food, it lasts until you need your next meal.

> Lord, how do people make it in this world without
> their daily manna from Your Word? My soul would
> perish and be swallowed up in a world that doesn't

care if I didn't have Your presence in the Holy
Spirit and Your Word as my road map through
this wilderness called the world. Thank You, Holy
Father. I lift my soul to You. Amen.

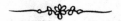

A Heart of War

The words of his mouth were smoother than butter,
but war was in his heart: his words were softer than
oil, yet were they drawn swords.
—Psalm 55:21 (KJV)

Have you ever had a person you really loved and respected hurt you horribly with words? Not words of encouragement or words of praise but words of deception and sarcasm? The mouth says one thing, and it sounds as smooth and right as butter being spread on warm bread. But you know the friend's intent and that the person is making war upon you in his or her heart.

The person says all the right things but in the wrong way. You've shared all your secrets, most intimate thoughts, and beliefs. These are stored in an arsenal to use against you when the time is right. You trusted this individual because you loved him or her.

A person can use soft-sounding words that appear correct on the surface, but the intent and end are destruction. At the appointed time, usually when it is most beneficial to that person, he or she draws from the arsenal of knowledge against you and uses it as a drawn sword.

This type of person can hurt you more than anyone else in your life because of your love for and trust of him or her. When the person proves to be an enemy, you hurt and grieve over the loss of one you deemed a friend. This is similar to losing one to death. But let me encourage you. It will end. Read the next verse of this beautiful psalm of David: "Cast thy burden upon the LORD, and he shall sustain thee: he shall never suffer the righteous to be moved" (Psalm 55:22 KJV).

Stretch Forth in Faith

And when he had looked round about on them
with anger, being grieved for the hardness of their
hearts, he saith unto the man, Stretch forth thine
hand. And he stretched it out: and his hand was
restored whole as the other.

—Mark 3:5 (KJV)

That man's right hand was dead and withered. It was deformed. It was useless. It had no power or life in it. It was paralyzed.

On another Sabbath He went into the synagogue
and was teaching, and a man was there whose right
hand was shriveled. (Luke 6:6 NIV)

That man lived with that dead right hand a long time. Human reason says the hand is dead. Faith in Jesus says, "Stretch forth thine hand."

If the man had not obeyed, his hand would have remained useless. He obeyed in spite of human reason because that is what faith is—obedience to Jesus in the face of human reason. His hand was made whole, good, healthy, and useful.

Religious leaders were not interested in the man and his need. They were interested to see if Jesus would heal on the Sabbath and break a religious law. Jesus was angry with the religious hypocrites. If Jesus tells you to stretch forth in an area that religion shouts no to, who will you follow? What will it be, religion, with all its human-made laws, or Jesus and His command to obey the truth in the face of human reason?

Is Jesus Christ stretching you in an area and religion is telling you no? If you listen to religion, you will remain dead, withered, deformed, useless, with no power or life.

What in your life that is dead, withered, deformed, useless, with no power or life is Jesus asking you to stretch forth in faith so He might bring it alive and make it useful?

> Lord Jesus, when You stretch me in an area that
> goes against human reasoning and protocol, help
> me be strong in You and to look beyond my human
> reasoning and rely on Your Holy Spirit power.
> Amen.

How Old Is Old?

The righteous pass away: the godly often die before
their time. And no one seems to care or wonder
why. No one seems to understand that God is
protecting them from the evil to come. For the
godly who die will rest in peace.
—Isaiah 57:1–2 (NLT)

Have you ever noticed when a young person dies, we never ask how young he or she was? We ask how old the person was. Old is not only gray, wrinkled, and halting, although it is one of the definitions of old. Old is also the age when the Lord retrieves your life!

What of a promise from Scripture to cover the young in human years or the godly in lifestyle who have untimely deaths in our human estimation? Is there one? Is God blind or unknowing of their deaths, or was there a purpose behind every one of them?

I serve a big God, and He has it under control even when I don't understand it. There is a purpose for everything under the heavens. No person passes from the face of this earth without my Father giving His approval because that life served a purpose.

If He takes note of the sparrow that has no spirit and is not fashioned in the image of God when it dies and falls to the ground, won't He make our deaths have more meaning and purpose?

There is a verse that soothes my heart when the godly are taken and I don't understand, or when the young are taken and I don't understand. God understands; that's why He gave the verse to all of us who need comfort at that time.

The righteous pass away: the godly often die
before their time. And no one seems to care or
wonder why. No one seems to understand that
God is protecting them from the evil to come.
For the godly who die will rest in peace. (Isaiah
57:1–2 NLT)

God takes you into his bosom when He protects you from an evil
you do not see or know. It is a blessing. Have we all not longed for that,
and not in a morbid way, amid our deepest hurt? How unsearchable
are His ways.

Lord God Almighty, only You know the exact time
to call a human spirit back into Your great heart.
Thank You that even if I don't know the reasons
why, You do, and I praise You for knowing exactly
the right time to call Your loved ones back into
Your Spirit. Comfort those who grieve with Your
Word and Your Spirit. Amen.

Epilogue

Depression and the Good Word

Anxiety in the heart of man causes depression, But
a good word makes it glad.
—Proverbs 12:25 (NKJV)

Depression has plagued me for most of my life. I have asked the Lord many times why I have to deal with it. I have asked Him to take it away. He has not. I have prayed for healing. He told me He would help me cope with it. Doctors have diagnosed the problem as situational depression and given their advice for its treatment. I didn't like what they prescribed. I prefer what God prescribes for me. His Word tells me how to deal with any and all situations in my life.

I do know the one thing that invites depression into my soul is anxiety. I do know the one thing that drives it away from me is to get immersed in the Word of God and stay there until He relieves it.

I write at these times, usually a poem about the verse or chapter that gave the relief I longed for. I think many creative people suffer from depression. How else could they write, paint, compose, or create if they did not know the extremes of human nature?

I have come to my conclusion for my life. Depression is God's way of bringing out in me what He wants to be said to the utter extremes of human living. It is to be accepted as much as the fact of my height. I can never change my height. I accept myself.

Following is Psalm 13 and a poem version of the psalm. I hope it helps someone to know God can use any aspect of human nature for His glory if you allow Him to. King David encountered depression at times when the situations in his life were overwhelming. He would look up to his Lord and cry out for help. The Lord hears the cry of a depressed heart.

> How long, O Lord? Will You forget me forever? How Long will You hide Your face from me? How long shall I take counsel in my soul, having sorrow in my heart daily? Consider and hear me, O Lord my God; enlighten my eyes, lest I sleep the sleep of death; Lest my enemies say, "I have prevailed against him"; Lest those who trouble me rejoice when I am moved. But I have trusted in Your mercy; my heart shall rejoice in Your salvation. I will sing to the LORD, because He has dealt bountifully with me. (Psalm 13 NKJV)

Cry from a Depressed Heart

How long, O Lord, will You stand by and watch my
spirit slowly die.
Will You forget Your child forever? You promised
we would be together.
I cannot see Your face, my Lord; it's hidden from
my sight.
I search for You throughout each day and long for
You at night.
I search about within my soul to find the
reason why.
My heart feels pain for You're not there, and
constantly I cry.
My enemy, my very self, exalts in causing pain.

My tears pour forth from deep within like rivulets
of rain.
O Lord, please hear, my God consider, I long to see
Your face.
Enlighten me, or I will die; please hear my human
case.
My enemies are laughing, Lord, they want to see
me dead.
They scorn me in my helplessness, heap insults on
my head.
But I will trust Your mercy, Lord, rejoice in Your
salvation.
My voice will rise in songs to You, proclaim in
exaltation,
For You have dealt quite bountifully in love
throughout my days.
The Enemy will not prevail; he will be destroyed
with praise!

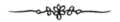

there was given me a thorn in the flesh,
—2 Corinthians 12:7b (NKJV)

Situational depression is my thorn in the flesh. It started when I was
very young and had to deal with the circumstances surrounding the
death of my dad. I have made peace with the fact it will be part of my
personality until I die or the Lord Jesus returns to take me home.

Depression carries a negative stigma in this
world. It is not disgraceful nor does it reflect
ones intelligence to encounter depression. King
Solomon was the wisest man in the world and had
bouts of depression living his life under the sun

in this sinful world. It is in his words, "Vanity of vanities, all is vanity." — Ecclesiastes 1:2 (KJV)

There is an end of death and depression. The Lord Jesus Christ has conquered them! Be comforted with His Word.

"For the Lord Himself will descend from heaven with a shout, with the voice of an archangel, and the trumpet of God. Then we who are alive and remain shall be caught up together with them in the clouds to meet the Lord in the air. And thus we shall always be with the Lord. Therefore comfort one another with these words."—1 Thessalonians 4:16-18 (NKJV)
MARANATHA!

CPSIA information can be obtained
at www.ICGtesting.com
Printed in the USA
FSHW011153020321